The GIRL Who RODE a SHARK

& OTHER STORIES OF DARING WOMEN

Written by **AILSA ROSS**
Illustrated by **AMY BLACKWELL**

pajamapress

First published in Canada and the United States in 2019

Text copyright © 2019 Ailsa Ross
Illustration copyright © 2019 Amy Blackwell
This edition copyright © 2019 Pajama Press Inc.
This is a first North American edition.

10 9 8 7 6 5 4 3 2 1

 Canada Council for the Arts   Conseil des arts du Canada    ONTARIO ARTS COUNCIL CONSEIL DES ARTS DE L'ONTARIO an Ontario government agency un organisme du gouvernement de l'Ontario   Canadä

The publisher gratefully acknowledges the support of the Canada Council for the Arts and the Ontario Arts Council for its publishing program. We acknowledge the financial support of the Government of Canada through the Canada Book Fund (CBF) for our publishing activities.

Library and Archives Canada Cataloguing in Publication

Title: The girl who rode a shark: and other stories of daring women / by Ailsa Ross ; illustrated by Amy Blackwell
Names: Ross, Ailsa, author. | Blackwell, Amy, illustrator.
Identifiers: Canadiana 20190088346 | ISBN 9781772780987 (hardcover)
Subjects: LCSH: Women—Biography—Juvenile literature.
Classification: LCC CT3203 .R68 2019 | DDC j920.72—dc23

Publisher Cataloging-in-Publication Data (U.S.)

Names: Ross, Ailsa, author. | Blackwell, Amy, illustrator.
Title: The Girl Who Rode a Shark : And Other Stories of Daring Women / by Ailsa Ross, illustrated by Amy Blackwell.
Description: Toronto, Ontario Canada : Pajama Press, 2019. | Originally published by AA Publishing, UK, 2019 | Summary: "Biographical vignettes highlight exciting adventures and innovative contributions of women and girls from a wide variety of countries and historical periods"— Provided by publisher.
Identifiers: ISBN 978-1-77278-098-7 (hardback)
Subjects: LCSH: Women -- Biography – Juvenile literature. | Girls – Biography -- Juvenile literature. | BISAC: JUVENILE NONFICTION / Girls & Women. | JUVENILE NONFICTION / Biography and Autobiography / Women. | JUVENILE NONFICTION / Social Topics / Self-Esteem & Self-Reliance.
Classification: LCC CT3203.R677 |DDC 920.72 – dc23

Original art created with digital media

Manufactured by Friesens
Printed in Canada

Pajama Press Inc.
181 Carlaw Ave. Suite 251 Toronto, Ontario Canada, M4M 2S1

Distributed in Canada by UTP Distribution
5201 Dufferin Street Toronto, Ontario Canada, M3H 5T8

Distributed in the U.S. by Ingram Publisher Services
1 Ingram Blvd. La Vergne, TN 37086, USA

For Rowan,
and my excellent mum—A.R.

* CONTENTS *

THE SCIENTISTS   46

Women who have voyaged from the deepest seas to outer space
in their quests to understand the world around us.

THE ACTIVISTS

Women who have dared to speak up, kick down barriers, fight injustice and make the world a better place — whatever it takes.

THE ATHLETES

Women who have pushed themselves to the very limits of their capabilities in pursuit of bold goals and ambitions.

THE SEEKERS   108

Women who have journeyed in search of meaning,
love, safety — the things that make a life.

* INTRODUCTION *

How do you help girls shape the world?

By showing them women's amazing achievements across the ages.

Women have adventured since our early ancestors began to walk. We've gone from Africa to Ancient Mesopotamia, across the Bering Strait from Europe to North and South America, in rafts and boats from Asia to Australia. Along the way, we've solved problems and slept under the stars. We've hunted, gathered and used the night sky as a map to guide us around the world.

It's time to get to know the stories of 52 women adventurers the history books forgot about. Some were living fierce pirate lives 2,000 years ago. Others are swimming with sharks and trekking through jungles today.

Together, these women show that being an adventurer isn't about being rich. It isn't about physical strength or being fearless. And it definitely isn't about gender. Adventure is within you. It's a way of seeing the world. For when you have no limits to your curiosity and imagination – when you are given an education, love and shelter – you can do anything.

I hope these women's stories inspire you to listen to your dreams and fall in love with our planet. After all, among all the galaxies in the universe, this world of frogs and fireflies and daytime moons is the only home we have. If you ever feel small, remember: adventure is within you. It's in listening to your own voice. It's going beyond your comfort zone. It's daring to be brave. If you ever feel like hiding from the world – remember that you are connected to every adventurer in this book. Really.

One of the first modern humans known to scientists was a woman. We call her Mitochondrial Eve. She lived in the grasslands of Africa about 200,000 years ago. Every person on the planet is descended from her. This means we are all connected.

We are also connected by what we are made of – stars. Exploding supernovas blasted the ingredients for life into the universe. Now these elements are what make up our bodies. That means we are all made of ancient suns. That means we are something close to magic.

Now let's get to know the stories of the women adventurers we are all connected to. Let's get to know what kind of magic we're made of.

THE ARTISTS

Women with boundless curiosity, gigantic dreams and a desire to share their amazing experiences with the world — in the form of writing, painting, photography, dance and music.

2

4

5

1. LADY SARASHINA
2. MARIANNE NORTH
3. ISABELLA BIRD
4. NELLIE BLY
5. ZORA NEALE HURSTON
6. FREYA STARK
7. EMILY HAHN
8. JOSEPHINE BAKER
9. MIHAELA NOROC

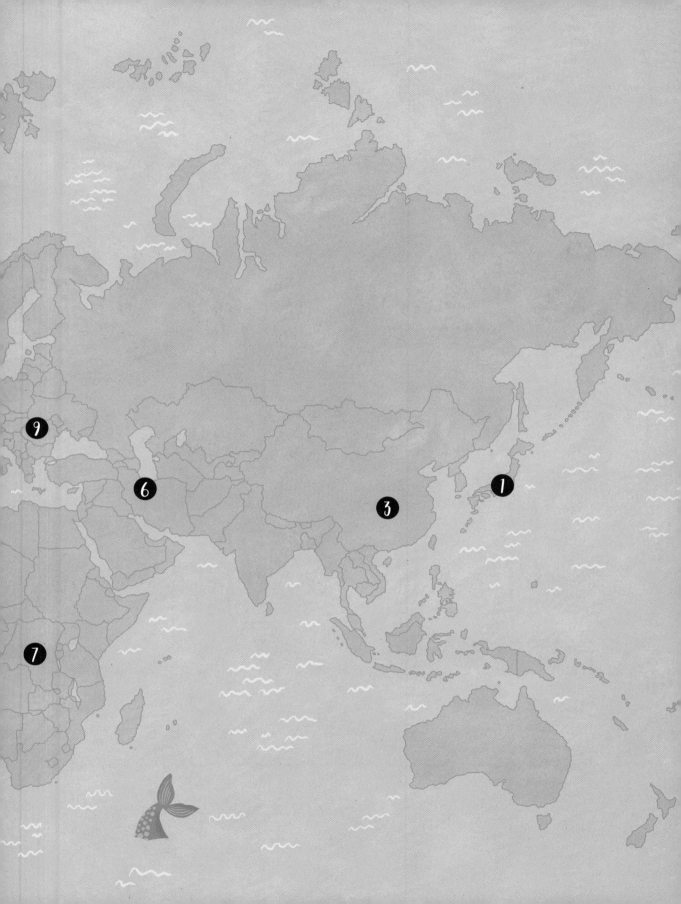

✳ LADY SARASHINA ✳

The lady-in-waiting who became the first travel writer

c. 1008, Kyoto, Japan — after 1059, Kyoto, Japan

A thousand years ago, wealthy Japanese women were expected to write and receive at least a few poems a day. In fact, a great verse could make or break a reputation.

What women could not do was hitch on a backpack and adventure wherever they pleased. They lived indoors, behind screens that stopped men from seeing them. They wore heavy 12-layered robes that made it difficult to move freely. To look beautiful, they blackened their teeth and grew their hair as long as possible. The only appropriate trips were to temples. Women were carried there in sedan chairs – tiny carriages propped on the shoulders of servants. From a slit in the fabric, they saw the world pass them by.

Sarashina got her first taste of life from a sedan chair when she was nine. That's when her family left the Japanese capital of Kyoto to live in the countryside. The journey was eye-opening. She saw mists cover entire landscapes, and bright moons rise over pine groves. She slept at the foot of huge mountains and drank sweet water from mineral springs.

Aged 31, with no other jobs available to a woman of her class, Sarashina moved into one of the royal courts. She became a lady-in-waiting to a princess, but the imperial world was boring. All anyone thought about was rank. Everyone gossiped. Everyone wanted to be close to the emperor. Sarashina wasn't interested in that world. She wanted to travel.

In those days, a young woman couldn't go off adventuring alone. Sarashina wrote in her journal that her mother refused to accompany her on trips. She had told her daughter, "Oh, how that would scare me! You had better wait until your father returns and let him decide where it's safe to go." Sarashina was frustrated that her mother was so old-fashioned. Why couldn't she imagine the beauty they'd encounter? Why were her first thoughts of being attacked by bandits on lonely roads?

Sarashina married at 36. This was practically old age at the time. While her husband was working in faraway towns, Sarashina went on trips to ever-more distant regions. She wrote about everything she saw, beautifully. Mount Fuji's thick cover of snow appeared like a white jacket over a violet dress. Streams of water bubbled like drops of crystal. Rolling hills looked like rows of folding screens decorated with paintings.

No other Japanese ladies left detailed records of their travels. There is nothing like it in other literature of the time. By writing about the thing she loved most, Sarashina became the first known travel writer. She didn't give her only book a name, but scholars call it *As I Crossed a Bridge of Dreams*. Japanese high school students still read about Sarashina's journeys today.

MORE JAPANESE WRITERS WHO SAW THE WORLD BEAUTIFULLY:

Sei Shōnagon (c. 966–1025 AD, *The Pillow Book*); Murasaki Shikibu (c. 978–1014 AD, *The Tale of Genji*)

"I went on one distant pilgrimage after another. Some were delightful, some difficult, but I found great solace in them all."

✳ MARIANNE NORTH ✳

The flower hunter who painted over a thousand plants

1830, Hastings, England – 1890, Alderley, England

Marianne North's days always began at dawn. She took her tea outside to watch the world awaken. Then she painted frantically outdoors until dark. After dinner, she explored outside till the stars glowed overhead. That was her routine, and she loved it.

Marianne was 26 when her father brought her to one of the wonders of the Victorian era – the Palm House at London's Kew Gardens. It was filled with tropical plants from every corner of the British Empire. After seeing giant African cycads, how could Marianne remain satisfied drawing English roses and daffodils? When her father died in 1869, she refused every man who asked for her hand in marriage. It was time to adventure, solo.

Marianne came from a well-connected English family. Ambassadors around the world wanted to meet her. Unfortunately for them, she couldn't think of anything worse than sharing 13-course dinners with strangers. For 13 years, she trekked through the jungles of India and Brazil. She painted the flesh-eating pitcher plants of Borneo and the redwoods of California. Her friend Charles Darwin told her about the amazing flora in Australia, so she went there too. Marianne wore the modest Victorian clothes of her time, but she broke every artistic rule in the book. To capture the bright colors of the rainforest, she didn't use "ladylike" watercolors. She used oil paints. And she burst them straight from the tube onto the canvas.

The world was dangerous in the 1800s. There wasn't just the risk of storms capsizing cramped ships. Tropical diseases could be deadly. Marianne became sick often. For weeks at a time, she was stuck in smallpox quarantine stations filled with thousands of others. Even then, she painted. She couldn't stop.

> "Did I not paint? – and wander and wonder at everything?"

After traveling the world twice over, Marianne returned to London in her late 50s. Now she planned to shake things up at home. At Kew Gardens on the edge of the city, she offered to build a gallery for her paintings. The director thought it was a wonderful idea. He disagreed on just one thing. Marianne wanted tea and coffee to be served to visitors. He did not. Kew was a place for serious scholars, he argued, not day trippers!

Today, the Marianne North Gallery is the only permanent exhibition in the world that's dedicated to the work of a female artist. No drinks are served. Still, if you look just above the gallery's elegant doors you'll see Marianne's cheeky nod to the director – perfect illustrations of coffee and tea plants.

MORE FREE-THINKING PAINTERS:
Georgia O'Keeffe (1887–1986, USA), Yayoi Kusama (b.1929, Japan)

RUSSIA

KAZAKHSTAN

MONGOLIA

CHINA

YELLOW RIVER

BEIJING

MIANYANG

YICHANG

NANJING

CHENGDU
MEISHAN
LESHAN
YIBIN

WANZHOU

WUHAN

CHONGQING

YUEYANG

SHANGHAI

LUZHOU

YANGTZE RIVER

* ISABELLA BIRD *

The Victorian lady who became a photojournalist

1831, Boroughbridge, England – 1904, Edinburgh, Scotland

Isabella Bird had suffered from back pain, headaches and difficulty sleeping ever since she was a child growing up in England. Her symptoms came and went. Nothing seemed to cure them. When she was 41 years old, her doctor suggested an adventure might do her good. It was all the encouragement she needed.

For the rest of her life, Isabella traveled the world. In Malaysia, she rode elephants through the jungle. In Morocco, she jumped on camels with local tribesmen. For Isabella, the best part of adventuring was being free of Victorian England's strict social rules. In 19th-century Britain, women could not even ride astride a horse. They had to ride sitting sideways, wearing skirts. To Isabella, this was ridiculous. It was like hopping on one leg when you could walk on two. So in Hawaii, she rode astride like everyone else. She wandered through avenues of palm trees. She climbed volcanoes and explored coral reefs.

In 1873, Isabella arrived in Colorado (now part of the USA). When she ran out of travel money, she cooked and cleaned for cowboys. It was a life far removed from the restrictions and drawing rooms of home, and it felt good.

Isabella wanted to share her adventures with the women at home in Britain. She began writing books. In them, she described the mountains of America's Wild West and the wide open skies. She described falling in love with a one-eyed cowboy named Mountain Jim. She described how freedom felt. Soon she was famous for her adventures. In 1892, Isabella was made one of the first female fellows of Britain's Royal Geographical Society. Many members resisted allowing women to join. One man even wrote to *The Times* about it. He argued that women simply could not "contribute to scientific geographical knowledge," and that they were "unfitted for exploration." Other women were banned from joining the society for the next 14 years.

> "Off the beaten track is the real world."

Isabella began learning photography in her 60s. Carting 20 pounds of camera equipment along China's Yangtze River, she rarely captured the sunsets or mountains. Instead, Isabella took photos of families, spearmen, traders, port workers. She portrayed China – and the world – as she really experienced it.

As for the illnesses that had troubled her since childhood? When she traveled, they disappeared.

MORE EARLY ADVENTURERS:
Annie Smith Peck (1850–1935, USA), Fanny Bullock Workman (1859–1925, USA)

* NELLIE BLY *

The superstar reporter who changed the world by writing about it

1864, Cochran's Mills, Pennsylvania, USA – 1922, New York City, New York, USA

How did a poor young woman from Pennsylvania end up becoming the most famous reporter in America? By insisting upon it.

Nellie Bly's story begins in 1885, when she was 21 years old. While working at a Pittsburgh boarding house, Nellie picked up a copy of the local newspaper. One headline in particular caught her eye. It said, "What are girls good for?" The columnist Erasmus Wilson said that women were only good for giving birth. He wished females would stay at home and stop taking men's jobs. Nellie could not believe what she was reading. She wrote to the newspaper. Women were just as smart as men, she argued. In fact, women should take *more* of the men's jobs! The editor was so impressed by Nellie's spirit, he hired her as his newest staff writer.

In the 1880s, women journalists were expected to cover flower shows and ladies' lunches. Nellie never followed that path. She exposed poor factory conditions in Pittsburgh. She traveled to Mexico and reported on government corruption. When her editor tried to push fashion stories on her, she quit. Her leaving letter read, "I'm off to New York. Look out for me." Nellie's name showed up in the *New York World* newspaper soon after.

Her most famous story was light and full of adventure. In the winter of 1889, she became the first person to turn Jules Verne's fictional story, *Around the world in Eighty Days*, into fact. So she wouldn't be weighed down by luggage, Nellie brought just one outfit – a dress, a black checked coat and a nifty cap. By ship and train, she traveled around the world. In France she stopped for tea with Jules Verne. In Sri Lanka she bought deeply dark emeralds, fire-lit diamonds and rubies like pure drops of blood. In Singapore she bought a monkey and sailed into the most beautiful thing she had ever seen – a monsoon.

While sailing around Asia, everyone on Nellie's passenger ship was rooting for her. One of the chief engineers even had written on the ship's engines:

For Nellie Bly
We'll win or die
January 20, 1890

Sailing from Japan into San Francisco, a high-speed train was waiting to bring Nellie back to New York. Riding across the States, whenever the train stopped in a town, she found herself in a cloud of fruit, flowers, loud cheers and wild hurrahs.

Nellie made it home in 72 days, 6 hours and 11 minutes. She had proved that an unprotected woman could travel the globe without fear. She had proved that guts can take you far. Most of all, she had shown that if adventure is what you want, you'd better insist upon it.

MORE ROUND-THE-WORLD RECORD BREAKERS:
Lady Grace Hay Drummond-Hay (first woman to travel around the world by air, in a Zeppelin, 1929),
Elspeth Beard (first British woman to motorcycle around the world, 1984)

* ZORA NEALE HURSTON *

The anthropologist who practiced voodoo

1891, Notasulga, Alabama, USA – 1960, Fort Pierce, Florida, USA

Zora Neale Hurston's mother always told her to "jump at the sun," but it wasn't that easy. Zora was smart, but she was also poor. As a young woman, she needed to work many odd jobs just to survive. That meant there was no time for studying. At the age of 26, she still hadn't finished high school. Then Zora remembered: "*Jump at the sun.*" She slashed ten years off her age and went back to graduate.

In 1925, Zora arrived in Harlem, New York with no job, no friends and $1.50 in her pocket. She studied anthropology at Columbia University, and she loved it. It was poking and prying with a purpose. Folklore especially felt like the boiled down juice of human living.

> "I love myself when I am laughing...
> and then again when I am looking
> mean and impressive."

Anthropology is the study of people and their cultures. Zora's first attempt at the practice did not go well. Encouraged by a college professor, she drove across Florida in search of traditional stories from African Americans. Unfortunately, her nice car and northern accent marked her out as different. Who wanted to share their tales with this fancy lady from afar? But Zora *was* from the South. She had grown up in Florida!

The next time Zora tried collecting stories, she decided to show her true Florida self. At rural railroad camps, sawdust mills and juke joints, she picked up her guitar and played the songs from her childhood. Then she'd say to whoever was listening, "Got any yourself?" Before she knew it, she was at the heart of the party, sharing music and stories with everyone around.

Voodoo is an African religion involving the worship of spirits. In Zora's day, it was seen by American politicians as a dangerous kind of black magic. It was made illegal. Zora went to the US city of New Orleans to discover its roots anyway. To gain the trust of those who practiced voodoo, she took part in some of their ceremonies. In one, she even had her blood mixed with a rattlesnake's. Zora traveled on to the Caribbean islands in search of more stories. In Jamaica she joined boar hunts. In Haiti she photographed an alleged zombie.

In Haiti, Zora wrote a novel. *Their Eyes Were Watching God* sank without a trace soon after publication, but she kept writing. When Zora died in 1960, she was not well known. She was working as a maid in Florida. A decade later, feminist writers realized how brilliant Zora was. Her books were read in universities. Her work became famous. Today, her books are celebrated by everyone from Solànge Knowles to Zadie Smith.

MORE EXCELLENT AFRICAN-AMERICAN WRITERS:
Maya Angelou (1928–2014), Alice Walker (b.1944)

"I always travel alone and
I am not frightened."

* FREYA STARK *

The flower farmer who explored Iran's Valleys of the Assassins

1893, Paris, France – 1993, Asolo, Italy

Freya Stark's parents loved to travel. She was carried over the snowy Dolomite mountains in a basket before she could walk. She called both England's moors and the Italian mountains home. But in her 20s, Freya's life felt narrow and lonely. She was running a struggling flower farm alone in northern Italy. She didn't know what she wanted in life. Then she met a rabbit-breeding monk who knew Arabic. He began teaching her the language:

إثارة (*'iithara*) – excitement
سفر (*safar*) – travel
مغامرة (*mughamara*) – adventure

Understanding Arabic as a second-language speaker can be difficult. There are 28 new characters to learn. Text gets read from right to left. Freya kept trying. She was so happy to be learning the language of her favorite book, *One Thousand and One Nights*. She wondered to herself, "What would it be like to experience the Arabic world in real life?" As soon as she had saved enough money, Freya sailed to Lebanon. She loved the Lebanese villages that lay like brown lizards under the sun. She loved the leopard-colored lands of Yemen. She loved riding camels across the desert. She loved meeting new people.

Freya's days were simple. She went for a solo walk in whatever city, town or village she happened to be staying in. She spoke with whoever happened to be curious about her. In this way, she made friends with peasants and Bedouins, tribal leaders and soldiers. In Damascus, Syria, she became pals with a group of women. In Baghdad, in the country we call Iraq today, she moved in with a family of shoemakers. She got to know people. Their lives, their loves, their interests.

For Freya, the lure of exploration was one of the strongest drives of the human spirit. Aged 37, she set off for a part of Iran that had never been mapped by Europeans. It was called the Valleys of the Assassins. In medieval times, the valleys had been ruled by a murderous prince. To Freya, it all sounded like a story from *One Thousand and One Nights*.

Traveling on foot and by mule, Freya crossed rolling seas of mountains. She traveled across pale green fields until she reached her destination. There, she took compass bearings and photographs. She wrote journal entries that would be published in a book. Then she created the first modern map of the Valleys of the Assassins, its mountains and fortresses. For her work, the Royal Geographical Society gave her an important award called the Back Award.

Freya never stopped learning, adventuring or being curious. The world brought her to life. And through her 25 travel books, she brought the world to life for her readers.

MORE TRAVEL WRITERS:
Rebecca West (1892–1983, England), Jan Morris (b.1926, Wales)

* EMILY HAHN *

The writer who walked across the Congo

1905, St Louis, Missouri, USA – 1997, New York City, New York, USA

When Emily Hahn was at college, her mining engineering professor told the class, "The female mind is incapable of grasping mechanics or higher mathematics."

To prove him wrong, Emily became the first woman to graduate from the course. Then she spent a year working in the "guys only" world of oil geology. She found it dull, so she moved across the USA, from Missouri to New Mexico. For a summer, she worked as a horseback trail guide. Then she moved into a mud hut in the desert and wrote greeting card verses for money.

Emily loved to say, "Nobody said not to go." She thought that was the perfect excuse for sailing to the Belgian Congo (now the Democratic Republic of the Congo) when she was 25. She lived with Twa pygmy people in the Ituri Forest. She volunteered at a Red Cross hospital. But Emily wanted to see more of Africa. Accompanied by several porters, she began walking east. She crossed logs that spanned narrow valleys. She waded through swollen rivers and marshes. She fought off flies that can cover a victim in blood spots in minutes. In the end, Emily walked 373 miles. That's as far as London is from Edinburgh! Finally she reached a nine-million-year-old lake, Lake Tanganyika, in present-day Tanzania.

In 1935, Emily moved to China to write stories for *The New Yorker*. She found an apartment in the noisiest part of Shanghai. She loved the life and color of her busy street. She loved the poets, artists and thinkers she met from all over the world. She also loved glamor. Emily dined with millionaires. She kept a pet gibbon, Mr. Mills. He was soon known for his mini dinner jackets.

> "I have deliberately chosen the uncertain path whenever I had the choice."

Emily had a serious side, too. With a Chinese poet named Sinmay Zau, she started an English-language magazine called *Candid Comment*. Through literature, the magazine encouraged an understanding between East and West. Writing was Emily's lifeline. When she broke her arm and was in a cast for a long time, she didn't stop telling stories. She just typed one-handed.

When Emily turned 45, she became a staff writer at *The New Yorker* and moved to Manhattan, New York. Every weekday morning, she left her apartment at 9:30 a.m. and strode to her office at the magazine. She continued this routine into her 80s.

MORE ADVENTUROUS *NEW YORKER* WRITERS:
Susan Orlean (b.1955, USA), Ariel Levy (b.1974, USA)

NIGERIA

ETHIOPIA

THE CONGO

KINSHASA

BOMA

KENYA

MATADI

PENGE

TANZANIA

KIGOMA

ANGOLA

ZAMBIA

"No happiness can be built on hate."

* JOSEPHINE BAKER *

The cabaret siren who became an activist and spy

1906, St Louis, Missouri, USA – 1975, Paris, France

Josephine Baker grew up in Missouri, USA. Her family was so poor they slept six to a bed. They couldn't afford Josephine's schooling – it ended when she was eight years old. By the time Josephine was a teenager though, raw talent was exploding from her every limb. She was working as a street-corner dancer in St Louis. She was recruited to dance in New York City. By the age of 19, she was in France performing cabaret on the Paris stage.

Soon Josephine was famous across Europe. She became so rich she owned a gold piano and Marie Antoinette's bed. She even had a pet cheetah named Chiquita. It caused havoc whenever it jumped into the orchestra pit at her performances.

After 14 years of dancing through the glittering Jazz Age of Paris, the fun stopped. On September 1, 1939, World War II was declared. The capital filled with refugees fleeing German soldiers. To Josephine, gold pianos no longer seemed important. She could have left France, but she didn't. Every night after finishing her shows, she went to a nearby homeless shelter. She made beds, bathed old people and comforted new arrivals.

When the Nazis occupied Paris, Josephine took a big risk. She decided to work for the French Resistance as a spy. If she was caught, she might be killed. Josephine wasn't afraid. She just laughed when friends said it was dangerous. "Oh, nobody would think I'm a spy," she said. Josephine went to parties full of important people. She gathered information that was recorded in invisible ink on her sheet music. So she wouldn't be caught spying, she even hid secret notes in her underwear.

In 1941, Josephine became even more ambitious. She traveled to Morocco. There, she pretended to be very sick, but it was a ruse. She was actually setting up a fake passport network to help Jewish refugees escape to South America.

Josephine also entertained French, British and American troops to boost their spirits. She refused payment for her performances. Her hope was only that, "When soldiers applaud me...they will never acquire a hatred for color because of the cheer I have brought them." It was an idea that would spark the beginning of her civil rights work in the United States. She found it ridiculous that in Europe and North Africa she was welcome in the palaces of kings and queens, yet at home she couldn't even walk into certain hotels or order a cup of coffee because she was black.

In 1963, Josephine was the only official female speaker at the "March on Washington" protest alongside Martin Luther King Jr. Looking out at the mix of races in the crowd, she declared: "Salt and pepper – just what it should be."

MORE JAZZ AGE ADVENTURERS:

Ma Rainey (1886–1939, USA), Zelda Fitzgerald (1900–1948, USA)

* MIHAELA NOROC *

The photographer who captures the beauty of women around the globe

1985, Bucharest, Romania

On holiday in Ethiopia in 2013, Mihaela Noroc saw some women working in big, modern cities. Others were living in rural villages. Some were rich and some were poor. Some were young and some were old. Every single woman was beautiful. That's when Mihaela realized beauty has no bounds. It's all around us. It's in a village, in a skyscraper. It's in Asia, it's in Africa. It's everywhere. Beauty is in two kind eyes. It's in a smile. It's about being yourself.

Mihaela left her job in Bucharest, Romania. She started backpacking around the world. Her mission was to capture the beauty of women around the globe. She photographed Guatemalan vegetable sellers and Greek science students, Icelandic pop singers and Amazon rainforest dwellers.

> "Women shine like stars in all environments. We just have to open our eyes."

How did Mihaela get strangers to agree to having their photo taken? With her friendly smile. With her kind eyes. By being herself. Mihaela can also speak five languages, which helps her communicate. If language fails, she just laughs and pantomimes with her hands.

Mihaela posted her photos online. Donations to help fund her travels began pouring in from people around the world. Her project became bigger and bigger. In 2017, Mihaela published her first book, *The Atlas of Beauty: Women of the World in 500 Portraits*.

In 2018, Mihaela visited one of the world's largest refugee camps. One million Rohingya people are sheltering at Kutupalong camp in Bangladesh. They have been forced to leave their home in Myanmar – where they are often attacked and killed for being Muslim instead of Buddhist, like most others. Mihaela also traveled to North Korea, a secretive state that citizens cannot leave. She followed the edge of war in the mountains of Afghanistan too. In all these places where people are struggling, she spoke with the women living there. She saw that our differences are what make us beautiful. They should never be a trigger for wars and hate.

Mihaela is still capturing the inner and outer beauty of women around the globe. Maybe your hometown will be next.

Would you let Mihaela take your photo? What story would you like to tell her?

MORE PHOTOGRAPHERS:
Xyza Cruz Bacani (b.1987, Philippines), Yagazie Emezi (b.1989, Nigeria)

THE PIONEERS

Women who have blazed trails from the mountains to the plains. These adventurers have broken big ground for the rest of us.

2

5

4

3

1 TEUTA
2 ISOBEL GUNN
3 SACAGAWEA
4 AMELIA EARHART
5 BERYL MARKHAM
6 ADA BLACKJACK
7 LUCY NABIKI TAKONA
8 AISHOLPAN NURGAIV

∗ TEUTA ∗

The pirate queen who stood up to Ancient Rome

c. 200 BC, Ancient Illyria

There were many pirates roaming the Mediterranean Sea during ancient times, but we only know of one who was a woman. Her name was Teuta.

Teuta's husband was King Agron of the Ardiaean kingdom. When he died, she took over as regent to the throne. Teuta wasn't the type to stay at home and wait for riches to come to her. She took charge of many of her pirate army's attacks. In one instance, it's said that she and her sailors docked their vessels just outside Epidamnus in Greece. They pretended to be exhausted as they approached the city gates on foot. Begging the guards to let them enter, they said they just wanted to fill their drinking jugs with a little water. The careless guards let them pass. A few minutes later, the sounds of ceramic jugs smashing to the ground rang through the streets. They had hidden knives in their jugs and were attacking civilians. They were going to pillage the city!

For a while, the Roman government ignored complaints about Teuta's pirate army. But when their merchant boats began to be attacked, Rome sent a pair of ambassadors to put Teuta in her place. The queen was furious. She argued that piracy was a lawful trade in her kingdom. How dare another nation interfere with this private enterprise! She had one of the Roman ambassadors killed because he annoyed her so much. This broke an international law protecting all diplomats from harm. Rome hit back by declaring war on Teuta's kingdom. This queen had taken on the most powerful nation in the Western world. Now she had to face an invading army complete with 20,000 horses.

After a year of fighting, Teuta knew it was time to surrender. She was a brilliant negotiator. Even though she had lost the war, she convinced the Romans to let her hold on to a piece of land and two unarmed ships. After that, this powerful woman was written out of history.

All this happened more than 2,000 years ago. Still, today it's said that Teuta's pirate treasures remain buried in the hills somewhere above the Adriatic Sea. They're just waiting to be discovered by some lucky adventurer.

MORE PIRATES:

Grace O'Malley (c. 1530–1603, Ireland), Ching Shih (1775–1844, China)

✳ ISOBEL GUNN ✳

The fur trapper who crossed the Canadian wilderness in disguise

c. 1780, Orkney, Scotland – 1861, Orkney, Scotland

More than 200 years ago, Isobel Gunn pulled off one of the most exciting feats of her time. She wasn't respected in her day, but her bold adventures proved that women can be as strong and brave as any man.

Isobel grew up on the remote Orkney Islands in Scotland. Most of the islanders were poor. They had to deal with crop failures, blinding storms and hard work out in the fields. Only the young men had the chance to create a new life for themselves. They could work for the Hudson's Bay Company (HBC), collecting beaver furs in the Canadian wilderness for £8 a year (about $5.00 USD) – a lot of money in those days.

Like hundreds of other local lads, Isobel's brother George signed up to work in present-day Canada. On trips home, he would have shared epic tales with his sister. He would have spoken of wolves and polar bears that attacked grown men, of furious winters and mosquito-filled summers. George would have told his sister about trading tobacco, brandy and guns with Indigenous peoples – all so that wealthy Europeans could wear fashionable felt hats made from beaver.

Isobel was 26 years old and unmarried. Her future did not look promising, so she decided to do something about it. European women couldn't join the HBC. The work was seen as too dangerous for such "frail creatures." So in the summer of 1806, she disguised herself as a man and showed up at the local recruitment office. She got a job using her father's name, John Fubbister. Unable to read or write, she signed her contract with an "X."

That autumn, Isobel sailed more than 3,000 miles from home. Through the crunching ice of Hudson's Strait, she arrived in the heart of Canada. Her job was to canoe thousands of miles along rushing rivers. She also had to carry backbreaking loads of supplies between trading posts. The work was dangerous, but "John Fubbister" was far from frail. He was as strong and ambitious as the others. In fact, he even earned a raise from his bosses for working so "willingly and well."

Isobel traveled to Moose Factory, Fort Albany, Henley House and Martin Falls. She managed to hide her gender from her bosses for two years. On December 29, 1807, at Pembina trading post in present-day North Dakota, USA, Isobel begged her boss to let her rest by his fire. That night, Isobel gave birth to a baby boy.

Needless to say, the heads of the company were shocked that a woman had been secretly laboring for them. Even though she was great at her job, Isobel and her child were sent home to Orkney. She worked as a poor mitten maker into her 80s – an incredible age in the 19th century. But then, Isobel Gunn always defied expectations.

MORE SCOTTISH ADVENTURERS:
Nan Shepherd (1893–1981), Betsy Whyte (1919–1988)

* SACAGAWEA *

The teenager who joined America's biggest expedition

c. 1788, Lemhi River Valley, present-day Idaho, USA — c. 1812 Fort Manuel, present-day South Dakota, USA

Sacagawea grew up in the Rocky Mountains. She was born to the Shoshone tribe. Then when she was 12 years old, she was kidnapped by a different tribe. She was taken hundreds of miles east to America's Great Plains. Four years later, she traveled back to the mountains as part of the biggest expedition in the history of the United States.

The Corps of Discovery was headed by Captains Meriwether Lewis and William Clark. Their job was to find a safe route to the Pacific Ocean. The group was better prepared than any expedition before them. They had canoes and horses. They even carried writing desks and a violin. But they still needed one thing: an interpreter to communicate with Indigenous people. They found their 31st official member in the winter of 1804 – fur trapper and interpreter Toussaint Charbonneau. Traveling with him was his young wife, Sacagawea, and their baby son, Jean.

On 14 May, disaster struck the group. A sudden wind struck the canoe Toussaint was steering up the Missouri River. Everything of importance was on that boat – clothes, compasses, books, microscopes. While the men panicked, Sacagawea calmly fished from the river everything that floated past her. Six days later she got her first formal recognition. A river was named in her honor.

Sixteen-year-old Sacagawea proved herself to be immediately useful as a provider of wild food to go alongside their meals of goose eggs, beaver tails and liver. She also acted as an interpreter and trade negotiator. She led the group through the mountains she'd known as a child. And she knew when to speak up for herself.

Near the west coast of America, the group heard that a giant whale had been washed up to shore. Sacagawea decided she had to see it. Captain Clark agreed to take her and a few of the men across the bay in canoes. It was the first time Sacagawea had seen the ocean. There, she stood at the water's churning edge – just her, the wind and the waves.

The Corps of Discovery team ended up traveling more than 8,000 miles into the vast wilderness northwest of the Mississippi River. They charted rivers, animals and plants in more detail than any other North American expedition before them. They created 140 maps. Could they have made the two-year journey without Sacagawea? It's hard to tell, but one thing is certain – this teenage girl did everything the men did, and she did it all while carrying a baby on her back.

For her bravery on that journey, today Sacagawea has glaciers, lakes and mountains named after her.

MORE WOMEN WHO HELPED CHART NORTH AMERICA:
Emma Willard (1787–1870, USA), Mina Hubbard (1870–1956, Canada)

HUDSON BAY

I.S.

SACAGAWEA on
L & C EXPEDITION

FORT
ALBANY

MARTIN
FALLS

PEMBINA

GREAT FALLS

FORT
MANDAN

HENLEY
HOUSE

MOOSE
FACTORY

FORT
ATSOP

NEZ PERCE

THREE FORKS

SHOSHONE

LEWIS & CLARK
EXPEDITION

SIOUX

ST.
CHARLES CAMP
WOOD

PITTSBURGH

PHILADELPHIA

WASHINGTON D.C

ST. LOUIS

SPANISH
TERRITORY

LOUISIANA

UNITED
STATES

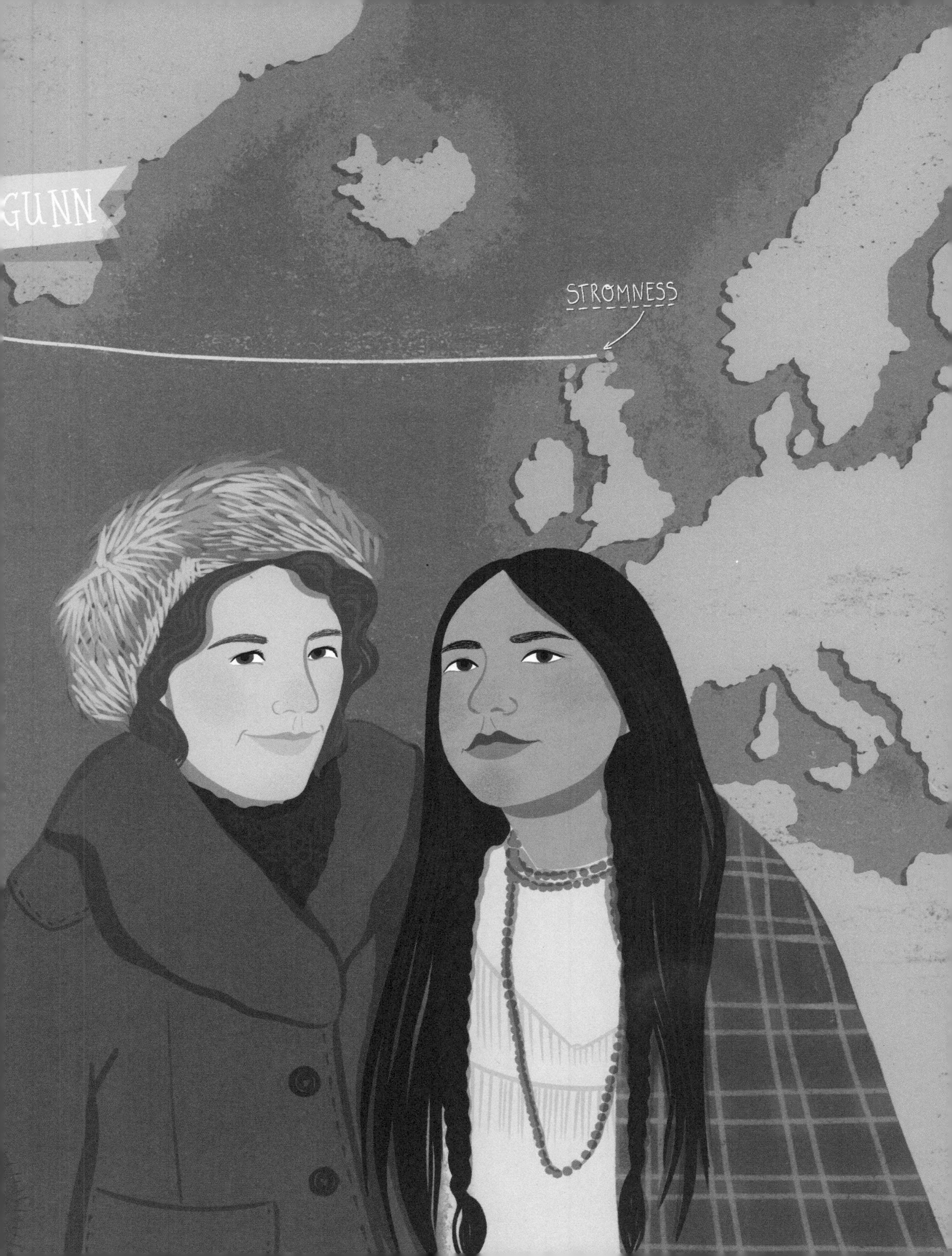
GUNN
STROMNESS

* AMELIA EARHART *

The pioneer pilot who soared over oceans

1897, Atchison, Kansas, USA – 1937, Pacific Ocean

When Amelia Earhart was a girl growing up in Kansas, USA, she kept a scrapbook. In it were all sorts of newspaper clippings about women doing big things in areas that were dominated by men. Amelia wondered what kind of career she would follow. Law? Film directing? Mechanical engineering?

In 1907, she went to an airshow with her sister. She watched a little plane swish and swoop in the air above. Watching its wings flash in the afternoon sun, she made her decision. She would fly planes.

Pilot lessons cost money. To save up $1,000 so she could pay for them, Amelia drove trucks. She became a photographer. She worked for a local telephone company. Finally she had the money for her lessons. Up in the air, she realized she had the entire world at her feet. She could go anywhere. On May 16, 1923, Amelia passed her final exams. She was the United States' 16th female pilot. To celebrate, she bought a brand-new leather jacket. So that it would look rugged and worn, she slept in it for three days! Then she cropped her hair short in the style of the other female flyers.

Amelia was known for her beauty. She also looked a bit like the first person to fly solo over the Atlantic – Charles "Lucky Lindy" Lindbergh. Newspaper journalists loved their resemblance. They started calling Amelia "Lady Lindy." They thought she should copy Lindbergh's stunt across the Atlantic! This was a dangerous task. The airplane had only been invented three decades before. Half of the pilots who had attempted the crossing had crashed. A quarter had died. Amelia flew anyway.

In a bright red monoplane, Amelia set off from Newfoundland, Canada. She had no radio. Her only company was the stormy blue sea below. After flying alone for 15 hours, on May 21, 1932, Amelia landed in an Irish field. A confused farm worker asked her, "Have you flown far?" She replied, "From America." The first woman to fly solo across the Atlantic, Amelia became a star.

"Adventure is worthwhile in itself."

Amelia went on to set all kinds of speed records and altitude records. In 1935, she was the first person to fly across the Pacific Ocean from Hawaii to the US mainland. This meant she was the first person to fly solo over both the Atlantic and the Pacific.

Amelia knew that setting big records could end badly. For her, the fun of flying was worth that price. On July 2, 1937, she was soaring high over the Pacific Ocean. She had completed 22,000 miles of her attempt to circle the globe. Then her plane vanished. Her disappearance is still a mystery.

MORE DAREDEVIL RECORD BREAKERS:
Bobbi Gibb (first woman to run the Boston Marathon, 1966),
Libby Riddles (first woman to win the Iditarod Trail Sled Dog Race, 1985)

* BERYL MARKHAM *

The pilot who broke an Atlantic record

1902, Ashwell, England — 1986, Nairobi, Kenya

Growing up on her father's farm in British East Africa, Beryl rarely sat still. She hunted barefoot with the Nandi people and wrestled with her best friend Kibii. She speared mamba snakes and had near misses with elephant stampedes. She was even attacked by her neighbor's pet lion!

Beryl's father lost all his money following a drought. When Beryl was 17, he moved to Peru to try his luck there, but she didn't join him. The hills around Nairobi were the only home she knew. To earn money, she became Africa's first female racehorse trainer. This was an unusual thing to do. Many British women back home still had to ask permission from their husbands or fathers just to go for a walk.

The period between World Wars I and II was the Golden Age of Aviation. The clunky, wood-and-fabric planes of previous years were being replaced by slick metal monoplanes. Daring pilots were opening up new routes around the world. Beryl wanted to be part of it. She persuaded her pilot friend, Tom Campbell Black, to teach her how to fly. At 29, Beryl became the first female pilot to work in Africa. She delivered mail and medicine to settlers in remote mining camps across the continent. She had no lights, no radio nor even the light of a village to guide her across the desert. Yet she flew for thousands of miles, everywhere from Sudan to Libya to Egypt.

Everyone hoped that one day it would be possible to fly from London to New York City. The pilot Amelia Earhart had proved it was possible to fly east to west across the Atlantic Ocean. Beryl chose to fly the other way, against dangerous headwinds, from England to America. To prepare, she started a tough physical training regime – running, swimming and horse riding every day.

The press couldn't believe such a glamorous figure was taking on this dangerous journey. Front-page headlines were dedicated to the "flying beauty." Beryl was not amused. She wrote a letter to the editor. She was flying not "as a society girl...But as a pilot – graduate of one of the hardest schools of flying known, with 2,000 flying hours to my credit."

By September 4, 1936 Beryl was physically and mentally ready for her flight. She took off alone in her turquoise plane with silver wings. Flying through the night, it was so stormy there was neither moonlight nor stars to guide her. The gales were so cold that ice filmed the windows and the engine broke down. She didn't make it to New York City. She had to crash-land in a bog in Nova Scotia, Canada. Nevertheless, she had broken the world record. She had proved "what every dreaming child needs to know – that no horizon is so far that you cannot get above it or beyond it."

MORE BRAVE AVIATORS:

Raymonde de Laroche (first woman in the world to receive a pilot's licence, 1910),
Amy Johnson (first woman to fly solo to Australia, 1930)

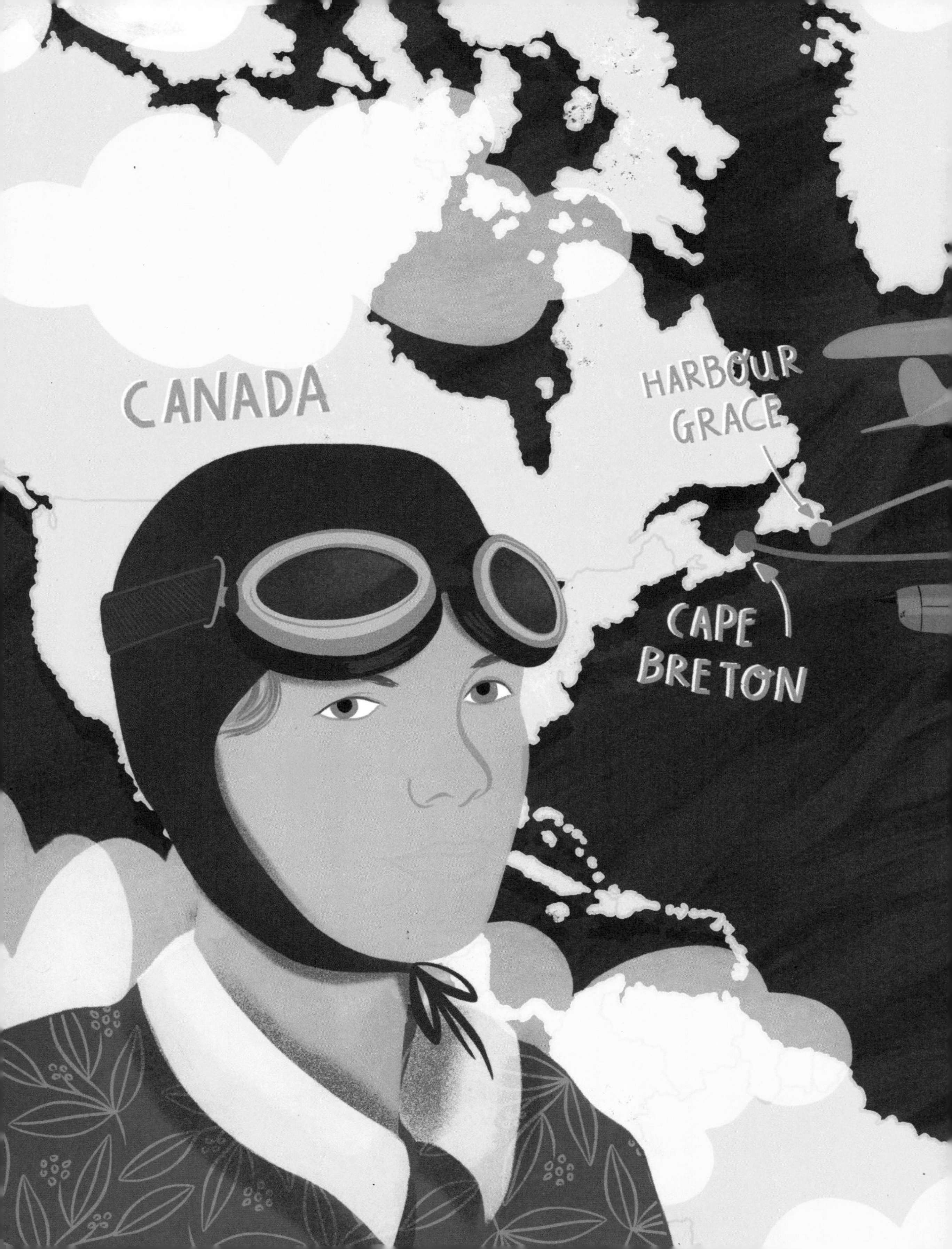
CANADA
HARBOUR GRACE
CAPE BRETON

* ADA BLACKJACK *

The castaway who survived alone on an Arctic island

1898, Solomon, Alaska, USA – 1983, Palmer, Alaska, USA

In 1921, Ada Blackjack was living a quiet life on the Alaskan coast. Then a group of young men came to town. They were going to set off on a one-year Arctic expedition. Would Ada join them as their seamstress? Ada was promised that her only task would be to sew winter clothes from animal hides. She would not have to hunt or do any difficult chores. It sounded like a great deal. Ada climbed aboard the ship bound for Wrangel Island.

Wrangel Island is a hundred miles north of Siberia. It's a world of ice and fog and polar bears. This close to the North Pole, there aren't even trees. Ada, Lorne Knight, Allan Crawford, Milton Galle and Fred Maurer arrived on the island's shores in September 1921. The group had plenty of rations like dark bread and sweets to see them through the winter. They hauled in driftwood and made blazing fires. The men hunted polar bears and walrus. Ada made hearty stews. Life was cold, but comfortable. Still, they couldn't wait till the year was up and a boat would take them back to Alaska.

In June 1922, a storm hit the Chukchi Sea. The water's surface turned to ice that no boat could smash through. The group was stranded. Their rations were all gone. Panicking, Allan, Milton and Fred tried to cross the ice to Siberia to find help. They were never seen again.

Ada's Iñupiat ancestors had known how to hunt and trap animals, but Ada did not. She had grown up going to a mission school. Still, Ada taught herself to trap white foxes. She shot seals for food. She picked nutritious roots, made driftwood fires and built a fishing boat from animal hides. She even chewed sealskin to make new soles for her shoes. Ada also tried to care for the remaining crew member, Lorne. He was suffering from scurvy. Sadly, in June 1923, he passed away. Ada was all alone. Each day, she prayed to God. She chopped wood. She shot at hungry polar bears prowling around camp.

"Brave? I would never give up hope while I'm still alive."

On 19 August 1923, Ada was resting in her tent when she heard a faint cry. It was a boat whistle! Laughing and crying all at once, she ran out towards the boat *Donaldson*. She had spent two years surviving on Wrangel Island. For the past two months, she had been all alone. Now she was saved. Now she was safe.

Back on mainland Alaska, Ada never went back to being a seamstress. She used the skills of her people – the skills she had taught herself – to become a hunter, trapper and reindeer herder.

MORE WOMEN WHO SURVIVED ON A DESERTED ISLAND:

Marguerite de La Rocque de Roberval (marooned on the Île des Démons for several years c. 1542), Juana Maria (lived alone on San Nicolas Island from 1835–1853)

* LUCY NABIKI TAKONA *

The female safari guide challenging expectations

1991, Naroosura, Kenya

As a young girl growing up in Kenya, Lucy Nabiki Takona loved the female teacher who taught her class. She dreamed of being just like her.

Then Lucy's father ordered her to drop out of school. He had arranged for Lucy to marry a much older man whom she had never met. Lucy was only 14. Afraid of losing her independence, she ran away from home. For three days, Lucy walked through the bush towards her aunt's home. She wasn't tired. She was used to traveling long distances to collect firewood and water. She wasn't afraid of lions or cheetahs either. Being taken out of school was what scared her. Lucy's aunt was scared for her too. She spoke with the elders in Lucy's village of Naroosura. Luckily, they convinced Lucy's father to let her stay at high school.

In her final year, Lucy's class traveled to the Kenyan capital of Nairobi. At the national museum, she was surprised to see a woman guiding people around the exhibits. Until then, Lucy had only seen women as mothers or teachers. It made her wonder what job she would really like to have. She had been fascinated by the animals of the Masai Mara her whole life. Why not become a safari guide?

For two years, Lucy trained at Koiyaki Guiding School on the edge of Mara Game Reserve. She learned how to track leopards. She practiced driving jeeps under the stars. She realized the importance of protecting the land for future generations. Now Lucy is the safari guide she dreamed of becoming.

Every day in the Masai Mara is exciting. Lucy's working day starts before dawn, when she picks up the visitors she'll guide for the day. The sun begins to glow over the horizon as she weaves her jeep through the grasslands in search of animals to see. Some days, she spots elephants grazing by the water and leopards caring for their young. Squabbling hyenas chase each other through the dirt. Hundreds of thousands of wildebeest tear across the landscape in search of fresh grass.

Until recently, only men have worked as safari guides in Kenya. Many of Lucy's male colleagues refused to believe women can do such a skilled job. One day, Lucy was racing her jeep across the savannah to check out a big cat sighting. The group radio was on. Her male colleagues were betting that she wouldn't get her vehicle through a deep ravine. Lucy *did* manage. One guide was so shocked, all he could say was, "Oh. That girl's tough."

Lucy *is* tough. She's built her own career. She's breaking down the barriers of traditional culture. She's an epic role model.

MORE AFRICAN ADVENTURERS:
Hafida Hdoubane (first Moroccan woman to become a mountain guide, 1994), Hamsa Mansour (attempting to cycle solo around Egypt in 2019!)

* AISHOLPAN NURGAIV *

The teenage eagle hunter bringing back a 2,000-year-old tradition

2001, Altantsögts, Mongolia

In the days of Ancient Greece and Rome, European women stayed at home to weave and care for their children. But on the grassy steppes of Central Asia, nomadic women were expected to be physically strong. Everyone hunted. Everyone rode horses. Everyone defended their tribe. And both men and women could find glory as eagle hunters.

When Aisholpan Nurgaiv's big brother was drafted into the Mongolian Army, she took on most of his farm chores. She was a little sneaky though. She turned her duties into time with her father's golden eagle.

> "Girls can do anything boys can if they try."

When Aisholpan turned 13, she asked her father if she could become an eagle hunter like him. He said yes. The pair found a tall cliff that was home to an eagle's nest. With her pink-ribboned pigtails flying in the wind, Aisholpan climbed the slippery rocks. The angry mother bird circled overhead, but Aisholpan still managed to catch a golden eaglet. She named her bird White Wings.

Aisholpan had chosen a great hunting partner. Female eagles are larger, more ferocious and stronger than males. Now she just had to train it to hunt. She crossed the Altai Mountains on horseback so White Wings could learn to scan the valleys for foxes and hares. She trained for hours in freezing −40 °C weather. She sang so her eagle would recognize her voice. She fed it by hand. In this way, White Wings grew strong.

In 2013, Aisholpan became the first girl to enter the Golden Eagle Festival. She and White Wings were scored for speed, agility and accuracy. They won the top prize! Some said it was because the teenage girl was a tourist favorite. They said it must be because the bird with the six-foot wingspan was exceptional. Actually, Aisholpan won on merit. A British film crew was there to capture her story. In 2017, *The Eagle Huntress* documentary was shortlisted for an Academy Award.

When Aisholpan is with White Wings, she isn't thinking about homework or checking her social media. She feels free. And she's paved the way for other girls to join her in the mountains. Two years after her win at the Golden Eagle Festival, two more female eagle hunters competed for the top prize.

These days, Aisholpan is creating new traditions. In 2018, she became the first person in Mongolia to go parahawking. "Parahawking" is a new sport that combines eagle hunting with paragliding. Aisholpan learned to cruise high above the snowy Altai mountains in a harness tied to a polyester "wing." Then she trained White Wings to land on her arm while she flew! Together, they soared.

MORE EAGLE HUNTERS:
Princess Nirgidma of Torhut (1908–1983),
Makpal Abdrazakova (c. 1989 – only female golden eagle hunter in Kazakhstan)

THE SCIENTISTS

Women who have voyaged from
the deepest seas to outer space in
their quests to understand
the world around us.

6

4

5

7

1

1. MARIA SIBYLLA MERIAN
2. JEANNE BARET
3. WANG ZHENYI
4. YNÉS MEXÍA
5. SYLVIA EARLE
6. ROBERTA BONDAR
7. NALINI NADKARNI
8. BOLORTSETSEG MINJIN

* MARIA SIBYLLA MERIAN *

The painter who traveled to Suriname in search of butterflies

1647, Frankfurt, Germany – 1717, Amsterdam, Netherlands

As a child growing up in Germany, Maria Sibylla Merian loved bugs. For her 13th birthday, she was even given a gift of silkworms. Feeding them lettuce, she watched in amazement as they changed from larvae to cocoons to tiny white moths. "How did they do that?" she wondered.

Maria's fascination with insects grew and grew. Her stepfather was an artist and, by his side, she began to paint butterflies. This was not without danger. In the 17th century, people believed butterflies were witches in disguise that curdled and stole butter and cream. Who would paint such evil creatures, if not a witch who must be put to death? Maria knew better. Aged 32, she published her first book about caterpillars and their metamorphosis. She wrote in German instead of Latin. It was important to Maria that everyone could read her book, not just male scientists who had been to university.

Even Maria's illustrations were totally fresh and new. Instead of placing butterflies against a plain background, she painted them next to the plant they drank or fed from.

In 1691, Maria and her family moved to Amsterdam. It was the richest city on the planet. Wealthy families kept curiosity cabinets filled with exotic wonders from every corner of the Dutch empire. Maria earned good money by painting the tropical butterfly and moth collections of the rich. But as much as she was an artist, Maria was also a scientist. She wanted to paint living creatures in their natural habitat, alongside their eggs and food sources.

When she was 52, Maria sailed with her daughter Dorothea to Suriname in South America. With its muddy swamps and rainforest where pumas lived, everyone at home called it the "Wild Coast." But to Maria, it was paradise. She even got to taste her first banana! The steamy capital of Paramaribo was surrounded by neat sugar plantations. Beyond that lay endless jungle. Butterflies as electric blue as peacocks danced. Giant silk moths swirled. Trekking among the macaws and kingfishers, Maria thought she was in the most beautiful place on Earth. She painted every insect she saw.

> I would "observe the transformation of all the caterpillars that I could find. I thus withdrew from all human company and busied myself with these investigations."

Maria's trip ended early when she became sick with malaria – a disease caused by mosquito bites. Still, she had already made the illustrations she needed to create her greatest book. *Insects of Surinam* featured 60 of her paintings. For her brilliant work, today Maria is recognized as the very first ecologist.

MORE WOMEN WHO STUDIED BUTTERFLIES:
Anna Botsford Comstock (1854–1930, USA), Margaret Fountaine (1862–1940, England)

RIO DE JANEIRO

MONTEVIDEO

STRAIT OF MAGELLAN

FALKLAND ISLANDS

TAHITI

SAMOA

FIJI

SUNDA STRAIT

MAURITIUS

CAPE OF GOOD HOPE

NANTES

CANARY ISLANDS

✳ JEANNE BARET ✳

The first woman to sail around the world

1740, La Comelle, France – 1803, Saint-Aulaye, France

Europe two centuries ago was a time before electricity. You could not travel long distances without great effort, and a pleasant life could only be afforded by the wealthy. It was a time when many countries and cultures were still unknown to Europeans, and a voyage around the world took years and was filled with peril.

It was into this world that Jeanne Baret was born. The daughter of poor farm workers in France, she grew up to be a herb woman like her mother. Her job involved collecting wild plants that could be sold as medicine in pharmacies. Through her work, she met the famous botanist Philibert Commerson.

In 1766, Philibert was asked to join the first French expedition around the world. His task was to find natural resources – medicines, spices, food – that might give the French an edge over other European countries competing for the biggest empire. Philibert knew of the perfect plant expert to bring onboard as his assistant: Jeanne. There was one problem. It was illegal for women to join naval expeditions. So, at the age of 26, Jeanne disguised herself as *Jean*.

Captain Bougainville sailed the group to its first stop: Rio de Janeiro, Brazil. Jeanne was warned not to go beyond the city walls – it was scary out there. A ship's priest had been murdered just days before. Lugging heavy wooden field presses and a compass, Jeanne went into the Brazilian hills in search of plants anyway. She found a brilliant one. Back on the ship, she showed Philibert a vine heavy with purple flowers. He took credit for the find, then named it after the ship's captain.

It was a hard life aboard the ship, and some men died from scurvy and tropical diseases. But for two years, Jeanne saw great beauty. In Patagonia, she walked among southern elephant seals that weighed as much as 50 men. In Polynesia, she saw the ocean sparkle as if a million fireflies were dancing on the waves. The glowing effect was caused by a kind of algae. She sailed over the Great Barrier Reef – a rainbow-like wall of coral limestone that stretched for 100,000 square miles off the Australian coast. On the Indian Ocean, she saw black and white creatures, like pandas of the sea, that no European had ever seen before. Philibert named them Commerson's dolphins, after himself.

In 2012, the first plant was named after Jeanne Baret. The *solanum baretiae* is a vibrant flower that thrives across South America. It seems like an excellent fit for the bold woman who explored the world in search of what she loved.

MORE FRENCH ADVENTURERS:
Octavie Coudreau (1867–1938), Anita Conti (1899–1997)

* WANG ZHENYI *

The astronomer who traveled across eastern China

1768, Anhui, China – 1797, Anhui, China

Wang Zhenyi was born among the sharp mountains of Anhui province in China. When her grandfather died, her family moved north to the city of Nanjing to keep her grandmother company. By the banks of the Yangtze River, 11-year-old Wang learned martial arts, horse riding and archery from the wife of a Mongolian general. But in the 18th century, Chinese women were not supposed to be "bothered" by studying. They were expected to do more "important" things like look after the home. Wang didn't see it that way. When she discovered her grandfather's giant library filled with 75 bookshelves, she read everything.

"Are you not convinced, Daughters can also be heroic?"

You may have heard the term "Renaissance man" used to describe a person with many talents, but how about a "Renaissance woman?" It's a label that suits Wang.

One moment, Wang was creating experiments in her garden that proved solar eclipses were definitely *not* a sign of angry gods – the next, she was writing poems that argued for equality between men and women. She described her ambition as "even stronger than a man's." Her interests ranged from astronomy to mathematics to geography to medicine. More than anything, she loved to travel.

Adventuring with her father to distant mountains and provinces wasn't just fun. She believed the experience changed who she was as a person. Even her writing style transformed. Wang was no longer interested in using flowery words. She didn't want to write about the scenery. She wanted to talk about real issues the rich were ignoring. She wrote important poems like this:

"Village is empty of cooking smoke,
Rich families let grains stored decay;
In wormwood strewed pitiful starved bodies,
Greedy officials yet push farm levying."

Wang understood the importance of helping everyone to get an education. As a young woman, she created mathematics textbooks designed for beginners.

Though Wang died at the age of 29, her ideas and inventions lived on for many years. In 1994, the International Astronomical Union even named a crater on Venus after her.

MORE AMAZING ASTRONOMERS:
Hypatia (c. 350–370 – 415 AD, Egypt), Hisako Koyama (1916–1997, Japan)

* YNÉS MEXÍA *

The explorer who proved science is for everyone

1870, Washington DC, USA – 1938, Berkeley, California, USA

"Just be yourself" is a popular saying, but what if you're not sure who that really is?

It took Ynés Mexía half a century to realize she was a flower-chasing daredevil. She quickly made up for lost time. She became one of the most dazzling botanists of her era, with 50 plant species named after her. She even gave her name to an entire genus of plants – *Mexianthus Mexicana*.

Ynés was the daughter of a Mexican diplomat, but her parents separated when she was nine. She was sent to American boarding schools in Philadelphia, Ontario, and Maryland. At every school, she was too shy to make friends. Still, she found comfort in going for walks to look at all the cool plants and animals. Ynés settled in San Francisco and worked as a social worker for two decades. Always, she felt lonely. Then, aged 47, she joined an environmental organization called the Sierra Club. She finally found other nature lovers to go on hikes with. Her confidence soared.

In her 50s, Ynés enrolled as a student at the University of California, Berkeley. She didn't care that in those days only young people went to university. On her first field trip, she tried plant collecting. She loved it so much that she broke her ribs while trying to grab a plant from a cliff edge.

Plant collecting expeditions weren't cheap, and Ynés Mexía wasn't rich. She wrote to schools like Harvard University and asked to be paid for the plant specimens she found. They agreed to her terms. Journeying everywhere from Alaska to Argentina, Chile to Peru to Ecuador, Ynés collected 138,000 plants in 13 years.

Ynés was great at what she did, but she was hiding a secret. As much as she loved collecting plants, she was also in it for the adventure. She especially loved being in Mexico's Sierra Norte mountains. She loved being out in the wild without electricity, lamps or even candles, "writing by the light of a fat pine torch." Ynés spent her retirement years climbing Brazil's highest mountain. She camped alone for a summer in Alaska's Denali National Park. She hiked through the Andes to the Inca ruins of Machu Picchu.

When she traveled with local guides, she rarely felt sorry for them when conditions were harsh. She wrote about one guide from the Colombian rainforest: "In the chill, overcast morning the old man complained that he had slept under a drip all night, but I did not care; why didn't he get up and fix it?"

No wonder another of her guides, José, said, "Another like the Señora I have never seen!"

MORE BRILLIANT BOTANISTS:
Beatrix Potter (1866–1943, England), Mary Agnes Chase (1869–1963, USA)

* SYLVIA EARLE *

The biologist who led the first all-women team of scientists to live underwater

1935, Gibbstown, New Jersey, USA

On September 19, 1979, Sylvia Earle set a world diving record off the coast of Hawaii. As she descended 1,250 feet beneath the surface of the Pacific Ocean in a special underwater suit, she switched off her lights. She wanted to see what it would feel like to be in a pitch-black ocean. That's when she discovered all was not dark. The fish surrounding her had little lights along their sides. Everywhere she looked, they made thousands of dancing sparkles and flashes. It was magic.

Sylvia grew up in the USA in a small Florida town with the Gulf of Mexico as her playground. She spent long days as a teenager investigating the salt marshes and the creatures that lived down among the seagrass. When she found a book on submarines in the school library called *Half Mile Down*, she was entranced. She knew then that she wanted to study marine biology.

On graduating, Sylvia began testing an exciting new invention. It was called scuba gear. It meant she could dive deep in the sea with ease.

In 1969, a new underwater research lab called the Tektite Project was developed. In that lab, scientists could live 50 feet below the water's surface for weeks at a time. The project was based in Great Lameshur Bay in the US Virgin Islands. In 1970, Sylvia led the all-female Tektite II team. She loved heading out of her underwater home to dive for hours among the coral reefs. When Sylvia wasn't researching and writing books about the ocean, she was traveling the world. From China to the Galapagos Islands, she explored the water.

> "Humans are the only creatures with the capability to dive deep in the sea, fly high in the sky, send instant messages around the globe, reflect on the past, assess the present and imagine the future."

Over 50 years of diving, Sylvia has seen the impact humans have had on the water. Every square mile of ocean contains 46,000 pieces of floating plastic. We've eaten more than 90% of the big fish in the sea. Sylvia's childhood playground, the Gulf of Mexico, now contains one of the world's biggest dead zones. An area bigger than New Jersey, 8,776 square miles, no longer contains enough oxygen for ocean life. This dead zone was caused by overfishing, oil spills, toxic waste, pesticides and pollution. There are more than 500 of these dead zones around the world, and half the world's coral reefs have disappeared. But this can all be reversed. Sylvia has founded Mission Blue, an organization which works to protect parts of the ocean called "hope spots."

Like the fish she saw in Hawaii so many years ago, they're flashes of light in the dark.

MORE MARINE BIOLOGISTS:
Rachel Carson (1907–1964, USA), Eugenie Clark (1922–2015, USA)

* ROBERTA BONDAR *

The astronaut who became the first neurologist in space

1945, Sault Ste. Marie, Canada

As an eight-year-old, Roberta Bondar was always putting plastic model rockets together. She thought being a spacewoman must be the best job in the universe.

Thirty years later, Roberta was working as a neurologist. This is someone who studies how the human brain works. One day, she spotted an advertisement in the newspaper. The Canadian space program was looking for astronauts. Roberta already had a private pilot's licence. She was the perfect candidate. She won a place out of more than 4,000 applicants.

For nearly a decade, Roberta trained for her mission. She exercised her body into peak physical condition. She put together ideas for science experiments. She spent long hours in NASA's classrooms, learning all about the systems she would operate. The *Discovery* mission blasted off from Cape Canaveral, Florida on January 22, 1992. Rushing up through the atmosphere was terrifying and amazing. Roberta felt like she was sitting on a Roman candle at a firework display. On board were six other crew members. Also on board were wheat and oat seeds, hamsters, mice, frogs – even crystals!

As a neurologist, Roberta's task was to study the effects of weightlessness on the human body. She conducted more than 40 important experiments for 14 nations. She also took photographs of Earth. Every 45 minutes, as the space shuttle orbited the planet, Canada's Arctic came into view. She saw the Great Lakes of North America. She saw her hometown. The images Roberta captured were spectacular. Roberta realized this: Earth is incredible. And you don't even have to wear a spacesuit to safely explore it. You can just walk out of your front door. What astronaut wouldn't want to explore this astonishing place?

Roberta also had lots of fun. One day, the first Canadian woman in space paid tribute to her favorite sci-fi movie, *2001: A Space Odyssey*. One scene in the film shows a floating baby, symbolising rebirth and new ideas. While Roberta was getting changed in the spacecraft's private galley, she floated around naked, just like the baby in the film.

Eight days, one hour and 44 minutes later, Roberta and the team touched down back on Earth. They had traveled 3,360 million miles. They had circled the planet 129 times. They had completed their mission. They had gone into space.

After her flight, Roberta became head of an international space medicine team at NASA. Now in her 70s, she works as an environmental activist and photographer. She fights to protect the planet she saw from space.

MORE WOMEN IN SPACE:
Valentina Tereshkova (first woman in space, 1963),
Mae Jemison (first African-American woman in space, 1992)

"I'm coming back to Earth with a feeling that there's absolutely nothing boring. There's no boring place anywhere on this whole planet."

* NALINI NADKARNI *

The dancer who became a treetop scientist

1954, Bethesda, Maryland, USA

The Brothers Grimm told stories of forests as dark places filled with dangers for girls and boys. Nalini Nadkarni has never seen forests that way. As a kid growing up in Maryland, USA, she loved climbing the maple trees in her yard. They were great places to hide from homework and household chores. When she was nine she even wrote, illustrated and published a single copy of a book called *Be Among the Birds: My Guide to Climbing Trees.*

Aged 22, Nalini graduated with a double major in biology and modern dance from Brown University in Rhode Island. After working as a field biologist in the rainforest of Papua New Guinea, she moved to Paris to be a dancer. In France, she observed many beautiful things that humans had created. She gazed into patisseries and at delicate shoes for sale in department store windows. Just a few months before, she had looked in equal amazement at the range of orchids and ferns that draped the tropical trees of Oceania. It was time to make a decision. Should she dedicate her life to the forest, or the stage? Nalini's nickname is the "Queen of the Forest Canopy," so you can guess the route she chose.

Since the 1980s, she's been climbing up to the treetops of Costa Rica's cloud forests. To get there, Nalini clips into rock-climbing gear – helmet, harness, rope. Then she climbs up. Dangling hundreds of feet above the ground, she studies the rare and little-known plants that cling up high.

Most of us see trees as static, unmoving. But to Nalini, even trees dance. She began an experiment to prove her theory. Among the giant red cedars of Washington state, she stuck paintbrushes to twigs and studied their movements. She calculated that a tree, helped by the wind, can "move" up to 186,640 miles in a year. Nalini wondered about people who might be seen as static. She thought about prisoners. In 2005, she helped to set up the Sustainability in Prisons Project. The project brings science and nature programs to prisons across the USA. Inmates work with biologists to care for threatened animals and plants like the Oregon spotted frog. They grow moss, keep bees, plant trees.

> "There isn't a person on Earth who couldn't use a connection with nature."

Professor Nadkarni is now on a mission to share her wisdom about science and nature with everyone. She's climbed trees with loggers, artists, musicians, clergymen. She's brought Alaskan Inuit people to the rainforest and gained insight into the world from their point of view. She's organized eco-fashion shows and created a Treetop Barbie doll. Her online TED talks have been watched by nearly a million people. She does it all for one reason: to help us find an entry into the natural world and rediscover our own place in it.

MORE WOMEN PROTECTING OUR TREES:
Wangarī Maathai (1940–2011, Kenya), Julia "Butterfly" Hill (b.1974, USA)

* BOLORTSETSEG MINJIN *

The paleontologist making dinosaur studies accessible to everyone

1973, Ulaanbaatar, Mongolia

As a kid growing up in Ulaanbataar, the capital city of Mongolia, Bolortsetseg Minjin was fascinated by her father's dinosaur books. Through them, she entered a world of eight-horned dinosaurs and plant-eating, pot-bellied, duck-billed giant slow-pokes. She learned that 70 million years ago her country was lush and humid. It was once filled with forests, lakes, rivers and dinosaurs. Now Mongolia's Gobi Desert is the richest fossil area on Earth.

Bolor's father was a famous paleontologist with the Mongolian University of Science and Technology. He studied dinosaurs for a living. As soon as Bolor was old enough to go to university, she became his student. One day, Bolor's dad was invited on a Gobi expedition with a team from the American Museum of Natural History. He persuaded the crew to hire his 23-year-old daughter as a cook. Bolor's studies hadn't prepared her for frying dumplings, so she spent her days collecting mammal and lizard fossils among the desert's red rocks instead. The other cooks weren't happy, but her amazing finds caught the attention of the expedition leaders. They invited her to the USA to study, so that's what she did.

While living in New York City in 2012, a newspaper ad caught Bolor's eye. It was for the $1 million auction of a rare dinosaur fossil skeleton. Bolor recognized which dinosaur it was immediately. It was the *Tarbosaurus bataar* – a cousin of T. Rex that's found only in the Gobi Desert. It must have been taken from her home country of Mongolia. Bolor reported the sale and the Mongolian president managed to stop the auction just in time. Since then, she's helped the US and Mongolian governments with the return of more than 30 stolen dinosaur specimens.

Bolor loves being at home in Mongolia. She loves camping in the desert and searching for new discoveries. She's so good at it that her team found 67 dinosaur fossils in one week. Her team has also discovered a 120-million-year-old *Psittacosaurus* dinosaur that's related to the Triceratops. They've even uncovered a new species of raptor!

Bolor believes Mongolian children need expedition experience, too. Why? All the adult paleontologists are retiring. No new generation has been trained to follow in their footsteps. The problem is, many Mongolian kids can't name even one kind of dinosaur. That's why Bolor set up the Institute for the Study of Mongolian Dinosaurs. It funds children's field trips to the desert. She's also helping set up dinosaur museums across the country.

Mongolia's first permanent dinosaur museum opened in Ulaanbaatar in 2016. The star attraction is the *Tarbosaurus bataar* that Bolor helped save from auction in New York. Now all Mongolians can see it. Maybe it'll even inspire some to train as paleontologists!

MORE PALEONTOLOGISTS:
Mary Anning (1799–1847, England), Meave Leakey (b.1942, England)

"Shouldn't the people who were born in this place help discover its own amazing past?"

THE ACTIVISTS

Women who have dared to speak up,
kick down barriers, fight injustice
and make the world a better place —
whatever it takes.

7

9

2

4

1

6

1 NAOMI WADLER

2 JOAN OF ARC

3 NZINGA

4 BESSIE COLEMAN

5 WHINA COOPER

6 GERTRUDE BLOM

7 SHANNEN KOOSTACHIN

8 NOOR INAYAT KHAN

9 ANITA RODDICK

10 SVETLANA ALEXIEVICH

* NAOMI WADLER *

The superstar activist making black girls' voices heard

2007, Ethiopia

When Naomi Wadler was in third grade, a boy touched her hair and said it was weird. When she came home upset from school, her mother comforted her. She gave some advice: "If it happens again," she said, "go the principal's office."

A kid did touch Naomi's hair again. So she went to the principal. She also spoke directly to the kid. She said touching her hair was wrong. It was dehumanizing.

By using her voice to educate others, Naomi grew in confidence.

When she was in fifth grade, Naomi came home from school crying. On that day — February 14, 2018 — a gunman had opened fire at a high school a thousand miles south in Parkland, Florida. Her mother held her in her lap. She gave this advice: "Be kind. Reach out to kids who seem like they're struggling."

Naomi heard a powerful political movement was happening across the country. To draw attention to the issue of gun violence, students from Alaska to California were planning walkouts at their schools. Aged 11, Naomi decided to organize her own walkout with friends.

A month later, more than 60 students walked out of Naomi's elementary school in Virginia. They stood in silence for 18 minutes. 17 minutes were for the victims of the Parkland shooting. The final minute was for Courtlin Arrington, a 17-year-old black girl who had been a recent a victim of gun violence in her Alabama classroom.

Courtlin's murder did not receive much media attention. "I knew that if I didn't speak up for her," Naomi said, "she would have become a statistic; she would not have been remembered as a real person."

"Real change starts locally; real change starts with you."

A news reporter was there to cover the protest. Naomi's statements about Courtlin went viral. She was invited to speak at the March for Our Lives rally in Washington, D.C. the next weekend. Half a million people were in the city campaigning for stricter gun laws. Naomi was nervous about speaking in front of so many people. But she got up on stage. She looked calmly at the audience. And she read the names of black girls who had been killed in shootings: Courtlin Arrington. Hadiya Pendleton. Taiyania Thompson.

Naomi said it was time to write a new story for girls of color. It was time for girls like her to shine, share, and have both a seat and a voice at the table. The roars of applause were so loud she kept having to pause her speech. Soon viewers at home were tweeting, "Naomi for president!"

Naomi believes we all have a voice. And there are so many ways to be heard. You can ask your friends to join you at a rally supporting an idea you champion. You can send a letter to a local politician about a cause you believe in. "Every time you advocate," says Naomi, "you are making a difference."

MORE YOUNG US ACTIVISTS:
Mari Copeny (b.2007), Marley Dias (b.2005)

* JOAN OF ARC *

The teenage warrior who fought for France

c. 1412, Vosges, France – 1431, Normandy, France

When Joan of Arc turned 13, she began hearing voices. Those voices told her that God had chosen her to save France from the English army. God had chosen her to help crown France's rightful king, Charles VII. Joan was a poor farm girl from northern France. Who would believe this was her destiny? Joan did. She rode a horse to the royal court to find out who was with her.

Speaking from the heart, Joan talked to Prince Charles about her task. The French army had been fighting the English on French soil for nearly a century. It was tearing the country apart. "Why not give this girl a chance?" thought the prince. He told Joan her first battle would be to win back the city of Orléans.

> "I am not afraid.
> I was born to do this."

Joan gave the English King, Henry VI, fair warning. She sent a letter to him. It said that if his army didn't back down, she would unleash a mighty outcry as had not been heard in France for a thousand years! The king ignored her letter. With that, it was time to battle. Joan dressed in a fierce suit of armor and cropped her hair short like a soldier's. Then, in March 1429, she roared onto the battlefield at Orléans. The holy voices told her not to back down, no matter what. When Joan's army felt like giving up, she convinced them to go on. After two brutal months, the city was theirs.

In town after town, the English army collapsed when Joan's army rode through. Victories kept coming. In Reims in July 1429, Prince Charles was finally made king. Things were turning out exactly as those voices had predicted. The French believed that God really was guiding Joan of Arc's successes. The English lived in fear of her.

While fighting outside the walls of Paris, Joan's luck ran out. She was hit in the thigh by an arrow and captured. Joan was imprisoned by the English and put on trial. Seventy charges were laid against her. She was accused of being a witch. She was accused of the crime of dressing like a man. Joan never backed down from her belief that God spoke to her. On May 30, 1431, at the age of 19, she was put to death.

A retrial 24 years after her death reversed the decision. Joan was found innocent of every charge. In 1920, the Catholic church made her a saint. Six hundred years after her death, Joan of Arc is still seen as a legend. She stands as a reminder to be strong and brave. She stands as a symbol to fight for what you believe in.

MORE WOMEN WARRIORS:
Anacaona (1474–c. 1503, Haiti), Takeko Nakano (1847–1869, Japan)

* NZINGA *

The queen who became a fierce fighter

c. 1583 – 1663, present-day Angola

Four hundred years ago, the country of Angola was divided into small kingdoms. The Ndongo nation was ruled by King Mbandi Ngola Kiluanji. His daughter was Nzinga.

Her story begins 23 years before she was born. That's when Portuguese explorers first sailed to the southwest African coast. Before long, they seized the Ndongo coastal strip. They renamed it Angola and built a city called Luanda. The Portuguese planned to create the biggest slave-trading port on the African continent. Forcing their way deep into the region's thick forests and savannah, the army ransacked entire villages. They ravaged the land. They kidnapped whole families. These slaves were shipped thousands of miles from home to the new Portuguese colony of Brazil.

To try and prevent Ndongo people from becoming slaves, Nzinga's father declared war against the Portuguese. When he died, Nzinga's brother became king. Recognizing his sister's intelligence, he sent Nzinga to Luanda to work out a peace treaty with the enemy.

When Nzinga arrived at the palace in Luanda, she was shocked to find the Portuguese governor in an armchair while she was expected to sit on the floor. What a power move! Nzinga glanced at her maid, who walked forward and crouched on all fours. Seated on her maid's back, Nzinga looked the governor in the eye and began to speak. With that regal gesture, she showed she was not a woman to be messed with.

When Nzinga was 43, her brother died. Nzinga was next in line to the throne, but women were not seen as fitting war leaders in Ndongo. To get around this, she changed her royal gender. She made herself a king, and had female bodyguards to protect her.

Well into her 60s, Nzinga was known for leading battles with a sword around her neck and an axe at her waist. She conquered the neighboring kingdom of Matamba. She promoted other women into powerful positions in her government. To strengthen her army, she offered safety to runaway slaves and soldiers. After decades of war, Portugal decided it could no longer fight Nzinga and her troops. They gave up all claims to Ndongo. King Pedro VI signed the peace treaty on November 24, 1657.

Today, if you visit the Angolan capital of Luanda, you might see visitors having their photo taken next to the statue of a fearsome female warrior. And now you know her name: Nzinga.

MORE TOUGH QUEENS:
Labotsibeni Mdluli (c. 1859–1925, Swaziland),
Yaa Asantewaa (1840–1921, present-day Ghana)

* BESSIE COLEMAN *

The pilot who opened the skies to everyone

1892, Atlanta, Texas, USA – 1926, Jacksonville, Florida, USA

Bessie Coleman grew up in rural Texas, USA, at a time when black people could not vote. They could not use the same water fountains as white people or even attend the same schools. Bessie's summers were spent harvesting cotton fields. She hated it. She'd rather be in class, learning math, but her family needed the money.

At 23 years old, in search of better opportunities, Bessie traveled north to Chicago and moved in with her brothers. By day she worked in a beauty parlor. By night she listened to her siblings talk about life as soldiers in World War I Europe. They said that in France there was no prejudice. Even black women flew planes. Bessie didn't want to paint women's nails her whole life. She wanted to fly. She began applying to aviation schools across the USA, but no one would accept an African-American student.

Bessie didn't see this discrimination as a barrier. It was a challenge.

Bessie managed a Chicago chilli joint, raised money from friends, and took night classes in French. On November 20, 1920, she sailed alone to France. Just outside Paris, she enrolled at flying school. Instead of taking nine months to complete the course, she took only seven. Completing a perfect figure of eight in her final test, on June 15, 1921 Bessie became the first African-American woman to get her international flying licence.

Back in the USA, Bessie applied to be a commercial pilot. No one would employ her because of her race. There was only one thing for it. She would have to work for herself. Using her newfound fame, Bessie entered the world of "barnstorming." This is a kind of trick flying that involves performing dangerous air stunts for huge crowds at airshows. Under the stage name "Queen Bess," she flew in loop-the-loops. She performed barrel rolls while the crowd held their breath. She did it all in the cool flying outfit she had designed for herself, complete with leather boots and a swish military jacket.

"The air is the only place
free from prejudices."

Bessie refused to perform if the audience was racially segregated. She took black women on passenger flights after her shows. She gave lectures to young black people and encouraged them to be pilots. Eventually, she planned to one day open the USA's first flying school for African Americans.

On April 30, 1926, Bessie died during a routine test flight in Florida. She was only 34. Yet by daring to dream, she lived on as a symbol of hope to millions of black people fighting injustice across America.

MORE CIVIL RIGHTS HEROES:
Harriet Tubman (c. 1820–1913, USA), Rosa Parks (1913–2005, USA)

TE HAPUA
TE KAO
KAITAIA
MANGAMUKA
OTIRIA
HIKURANGI
WAIPU
KAIWAKA
WELLSFORD
OREWA
NORTHCOTE
AUCKLAND
NGARUAWAHIA
KIHIKIHI
OTOROHANGA
TE KUITI
TAUMARUNUI
RAURIMU
RAETIHI
WHANGANUI
RATANA
BULLS
PALMERSTON NORTH
SHANNON
OTAKI
PORIRUA
WELLINGTON

AUSTRALIA
NEW ZEALAND

"I never waited for a
husband to do things.
I'd do them myself."

* WHINA COOPER *

The Māori activist who marched 600 miles for land rights

1895, Hokianga, New Zealand — 1994, Panguru, New Zealand

As a kid, Whina Cooper was often found at the *marae* meeting house at the heart of Māori tribal life. Sitting by her father's side, she listened in as elders debated important issues.

Whina's father was a chief of the Ngāpuhi tribe. He recognized his daughter's intelligence and favored her over her brothers. By the time Whina was a young woman, she was known for her *ihi*, a quality of authority which inspires awe. Māori women in the early 20th century were not expected to speak publicly on the *marae*. Whina refused to follow that tradition. When a male elder questioned her presence, she had the perfect response: "All men...the King, the Governor, the big chiefs...they all come out of a woman. Without women they wouldn't even be alive."

Over the years, Whina had many jobs. She worked as a rugby coach, a postmaster and a shopkeeper. She was a school teacher, an animal breeder and a gum digger so tough she was nicknamed "the Amazon Excavator." However, she was best known as a leader. She organized her first protest when she was 18. Later she helped found the Māori Women's Welfare League. It gave Indigenous women a forum where their voices could be heard.

Most famously of all, on September 14, 1975, Whina led a 621-mile *hikoi* march across North Island for land rights. The total area of New Zealand is 66 million acres. After 135 years of British colonization, the Māori share of that total had dropped to 2.5 million acres. Whina believed that if this process continued, the Māori would become a landless people. Without land, Māori people would lose their cultural identity.

Whina was 79 at the time of the march. She had arthritis which made her joints swell up painfully. She walked with a cane. Still, she walked. When she couldn't go any further, she accepted car rides to the next *marae*. Each night, in each new village, she led discussions about the importance of land rights. More and more people joined the peaceful march. By the time the group reached the capital on October 13, 5,000 protestors were chanting, "Not one more acre of Māori land!" Whina presented the prime minister, Bill Rowling, with a memorial of rights from 200 Māori elders. She also handed him a land rights petition signed by 60,000 people. The march alerted people across New Zealand to what was happening to Māori land. More protests were organized.

On her 98th birthday, Whina said her last wish was to see love between two races in New Zealand. With that, she shows us what dignity looks like. She shows us what it looks like to take a stand for your community and the planet.

MORE ACTIVISTS:
Fannie Hamer (1917–1977, USA), Ani Pachen (1933–2002, Tibet)

"We cannot help others... ...if we destroy their hab...

* GERTRUDE BLOM *

The anthropologist who became one of the first environmental activists

1901, Wimmis, Switzerland – 1993, San Cristóbal de las Casas, Mexico

Five hundred years ago, Indigenous Lacandón people fled Spanish invaders by hiding deep in the Mexican rainforest. They did not want to be colonized, to lose their traditions and their faith. Over time, they became the most isolated people in Mexico. It was into this hidden world, in 1943, that a Swiss woman came.

Gertrude Blom was a journalist who had spent the 1930s reporting on rising Nazi violence in Germany. When she was arrested and kicked out of the country, she joined the mass movement of political refugees being welcomed to Mexico by president Lázaro Cárdenas. In Mexico City, Gertrude made friends with artists like Frida Kahlo. She found a job with the Ministry of Labor as a social worker, studying and reporting on the working conditions of Mexican women.

A few years after her arrival, Gertrude heard about a team heading into the Lacandón rainforest on horseback. Always on the lookout for an adventure, she convinced a government minister to let her join the expedition. She had never ridden a horse before, but that didn't scare her. Her trip marked the beginning of a lifelong relationship with the Lacandón people.

Gertrude became best friends with the spiritual leader Chan K'in Viejo. She helped uncover ancient Maya pyramids. Among the forest's bright flowers and waterfalls, she listened to what the Lacandón people had to say. They said they didn't want outside ideas to take over their way of life. But by the 1970s, both the rainforest and Lacandón culture were under severe threat.

Loggers wanted to turn the trees into furniture. Ranchers wanted to destroy the forest so cattle could graze on the land. Settlers wanted to build houses, roads, electricity lines. Petroleum companies dreamed of the money they could make drilling for oil. The government supported all of this activity. It would be good for the nation, they said.

The Lacandón people were terrified by what was happening to their only home. They said, "It was prettier before, when there were no lights, no roads, only the sounds of birds. Now there are roads, and the trucks scare the animals away."

Gertrude wanted to help. She launched a tree nursery that's provided thousands of free trees for reforestation. She wrote hundreds of newspaper articles. She spoke on television. She published upsetting images of Lacandón people standing on newly cleared land, their only home gone. Her photos asked, "Is all this destruction, just for beef and oil and mahogany, worth it?"

In 1978, the government finally recognized the Lacandón people's ownership of the rainforest and created a special reserve to protect it. Still, the fight is far from over. Only 10% of the original rainforest remains. The Lacandón people are at risk. The struggle to stop deforestation and preserve their ecosystem continues.

MORE ANTHROPOLOGISTS:
Zelia Nuttall (1857–1933, USA), Jane Goodall (b.1934, England)

* SHANNEN KOOSTACHIN *

The girl who dreamed of safe and comfy schools for everyone

1994, Attawapiskat, Ontario, Canada – 2010, Temagami, Ontario, Canada

Shannen Koostachin loved camping by the shores of James Bay with her family each spring. Eating wild goose by the fire, listening to her elders' stories and playing in the spruce woods with her siblings was so much fun.

But as much as Shannen loved camping, she also loved learning. The problem was, at 13 years old she had never seen a real school. The children living on the Cree reserve of Attawapiskat were taught in run-down portables. Ceilings leaked. Pipes froze. Furious winter winds blew through cracks in the walls. Mice ran across the kids' snacks. And children were dropping out of school by grade four.

> "School is a time for dreams, every kid deserves this."

For ten years, Shannen's community had been promised that a real grade school was coming. But in November 2007, that promise was broken. The government said there was no money in the budget for a new building.

Shannen and her classmates were crushed. Canada was one of the richest countries in the world. How could there be no money for a new school? Using tools like Facebook and YouTube, they asked kids across the country to write to the government demanding that reserve children get "safe and comfy" schools. Soon tens of thousands of letters were arriving at the Canadian parliament.

Shannen gave speeches at rallies and youth conferences. She went to the capital city of Ottawa to speak with the Indian Affairs minister directly. She told him she wished her brothers and sisters had a classroom as nice as his office! She became the voice of the biggest youth-led children's rights campaign in Canadian history. At age 14, she was nominated for the International Children's Peace Prize.

When it was time to attend high school, Shannen realized she could not get the education she needed on the reserve. She left her family and home to go to school in the town of Temiskaming Shores. It was a two-hour plane ride, a five-hour train ride and a four-hour drive away. At its "safe and comfy" school, Shannen thrived. She was even asked to be the lead dancer in the school powwow. Sadly, just days before the performance, she was killed in a car accident.

In 2012, the Canadian parliament voted in favor of "Shannen's Dream." This motion was a promise to invest as much in the education of First Nations children as in that of every other child in Canada. That funding gap still exists, but other activists continue to pressure the government to keep its word. And Shannen's efforts made a real change in her community. Today the children of Attawapiskat go to a real grade school, with a real library and a real playground.

MORE ACTIVISTS FOR EDUCATION:
Payal Jangid (b.2002, India), Muzoon Almellehan (b.1999, Syria)

* NOOR INAYAT KHAN *

The Indian princess who became a secret agent

1914, Moscow, Russia – 1944, Dachau, Germany

Noor Inayat Khan's upbringing spanned the globe. Her father was Indian royalty. Her mother was American. Noor was born in Russia. Then she was raised in France!

Noor was writing children's stories at home in Paris when World War II broke out in 1939. She had been raised to be a pacifist. This means she didn't believe in violence or war. However, she *did* believe it would be a crime not to stand up to the Nazis. Noor fled to London and trained as a wireless operator. Her male supervisors didn't think she could send and receive important radio messages. They said she was too much of a "splendid, vague, dreamy creature, far too conspicuous."

"Liberté!"

Noor was signed up to the Special Operations Executive spy squad anyway. The British Prime Minister Winston Churchill charged her team with "setting Europe ablaze." The posting was so dangerous she was given a life expectancy of six weeks and a suicide pill in case she was captured.

Noor landed near Paris on June 16, 1943. Within a few weeks of her arrival, Noor's entire spy ring was arrested. She was the only person left operating. Her supervisors urged her to return to London, but she refused to stop broadcasting. Noor was now the most wanted person in Paris. For nearly four months, she traveled between safe houses in disguise. In October 1943, she was betrayed by a double agent and captured by the Nazis.

Proving she was far from dreamy, Noor tried to escape from Gestapo headquarters by unscrewing the bars of her cell's skylight. She hid the plaster damage with makeup. She connected a rope made of sheets and blankets to the rooftop next door. When she was caught, she refused to sign a contract promising she'd make no further escape attempts. Noor was now classified as "highly dangerous."

Noor was taken to a prison in Germany. She was kept in isolation for ten months. She suffered terrible beatings. Still, she refused to give the Nazis a single piece of information.

On September 13, 1944, Noor Inayat Khan and three other female agents were moved to Dachau concentration camp. They were shot that morning. Noor's final word was this:

"*Liberté!*"

Freedom.

MORE WORLD WAR II SPIES:
Virginia Hall (1906–1982, USA), Krystyna Skarbek (1908–1952, Poland)

* ANITA RODDICK *

The entrepreneur who traveled the world to create ethical cosmetics

1942, Littlehampton, England — 2007, Chichester, England

Anita Roddick grew up helping in her parents' cafe in the English seaside town of Littlehampton. Then she studied teaching in Bath. But the world beyond England was calling. While Anita was backpacking through the Polynesian islands in her 20s, she saw women rubbing cocoa butter into their bodies. Their skin *glowed*. Anita wondered, "What if natural beauty products like this were brought home?"

This was a wild idea. At the time, most British beauty products were full of chemicals and made in factories. Anita's were totally fresh. Her first products were based on natural ingredients and made at her kitchen table. They were not tested on animals. They were fair trade. Anita didn't have much money to set up a business, so she took out a £4,000 bank loan (about $10,000 USD). In Brighton, the only shop she could afford to rent was so grubby she had to paint the walls green to hide the mold!

The Body Shop's products were exactly what the young women of the 1970s were looking for. Anita opened two more successful stores in Brighton. Other young women helped to open more shops. The Body Shop became a familiar name around the globe. The color of its logo? Green.

Anita traveled for five months of every year to search out new beauty products. She saw up close how poverty devastates the lives of billions of people around the world. She wanted to boost projects that keep a community together and earn locals money. That's why she set up an organic farm cooperative in Nicaragua, health and education projects in India, a healthcare startup in Nepal and more.

By the 1990s, Anita was the fourth-richest woman in Britain. In 2006, The Body Shop was sold to L'Oréal. Anita made £118 million out of the deal (about $217 million USD). People said she had sold out. But she didn't buy a yacht or a big mansion with her millions. She founded Children on the Edge, a charity which helps disadvantaged children in Eastern Europe, Asia and Africa. Anita showed that a business can turn a major profit and still be ethical. When Anita died in 2007, she left her £51 million fortune (about $102 million USD) to charity.

She also left this powerful message to girls: You're never too small or powerless to start making a difference to your life and the lives of others. You can start by reading the books on your parents' shelves. You can ask your grandparents to tell you stories, then share those tales with a friend. You can walk around art galleries and spend time in libraries.

"Creativity comes by breaking the rules," said Anita. So be different. Be daring. Be yourself.

MORE AMAZING ENTREPRENEURS:
Tavi Gevinson (b.1996, USA), Gertrude Boyle (b.1924, Germany)

"Travel, for me, isn't just about business: There's the splendor it holds as a university without walls."

"Reality has always attracted me like a magnet, tortured and hypnotized me."

* SVETLANA ALEXIEVICH *

The Nobel Prize winner giving a voice to the survivors of conflict and disaster

1948, Stanislav, present-day Ukraine

From 1922 until 1991, the Soviet Union stretched across much of Europe and Asia. It was the biggest country to ever exist, and included present-day Russia, Ukraine, Belarus and lots of other countries. Its capital was Moscow.

Svetlana Alexievich grew up in what's now Belarus, just after World War II. No one had much money, and even staple foods like bread were in short supply.

Svetlana would often stay up late and listen to the women in her village share stories from the war. By the age of five, she knew she wanted to tell other people's stories. When she finished high school she worked as a local newspaper reporter. Then she moved to the Belarussian capital of Minsk to study journalism. Svetlana wrote poetry, plays, essays. But what she was looking for was a new style of writing – one that could capture a time, an event, people, emotions. What she wanted was a way to tell the truth about humankind. Svetlana decided to interview ordinary people and record their stories. There was one problem. A tape recorder would cost her three months' salary. She could never afford it. Luckily, some journalist friends pooled together to lend her the money.

For her first big project, Svetlana traveled thousands of miles across the Soviet Union. She recorded the stories of women who had seen action in World War II. More than a million had acted on the front line as nurses and doctors, but also as pilots, tank drivers, snipers. Svetlana wasn't interested in hearing about their victories. She wanted to know about the emotions a woman goes through in war. She wanted to tell the truth – to show how it feels to walk through a field covered with dead bodies scattered like potatoes.

War's Unwomanly Face sat in a publishing house in Minsk for two years. Svetlana's editors were worried it de-glorified the achievements of Soviet war heroines. This was a dangerous charge at the time. But when the book was finally published in 1985, it became a sensation. Two million copies were sold. People were desperate to know the truth about war, and life.

Svetlana used her newfound fame to travel to Afghanistan. The Soviet Union had been fighting Afghan rebels there since 1979. While rockets fired, tanks destroyed villages, and attack helicopters swung over the snowy valleys, she interviewed hundreds of officers and soldiers. She spoke to widows and the mothers of war victims. In her book, the pointlessness of war was unveiled. Soviet soldiers were shown as scared, confused boys. When the book was published in 1989, the Soviet government was angry with Svetlana. She was accused of telling lies about the Soviet army. A court case against her opened in Minsk. Called as a witness, a soldier's mother said, "I hate you! I don't need your scary truth."

Svetlana won the case. In 2015 she also won the Nobel Prize for Literature.

MORE GAME-CHANGING JOURNALISTS:
Marie Colvin (1956–2012, USA), Christina Lamb (b.1965, England)

THE ATHLETES

Women who have pushed themselves to the very limits of their capabilities in pursuit of bold goals and ambitions.

1. ANNIE LONDONDERRY
2. DIANA NYAD
3. CHERYL STRAYED
4. KIMI WERNER
5. SILVANA LIMA
6. ARUNIMA SINHA
7. MIRA RAI
8. LAURA DEKKER
9. ASHIMA SHIRAISHI
10. JADE HAMEISTER

✳ ANNIE LONDONDERRY ✳

The first woman to circumnavigate the world by bicycle

1870, Riga, Latvia – 1947, New York City, New York, USA

The first bicycle was designed in 1817. It changed so many women's lives. In fact, the suffragettes believed it gave women more freedom than any other invention. Before bicycles, women had to go about on foot, in carriages, or by riding sidesaddle on a horse. They always had to be accompanied. Now, they could go wherever they wanted, *whenever* they wanted. They could feel free.

Annie Cohen Kopchovsky loved feeling free. She was one of the USA's "New Women." These early feminists didn't stay at home. They pushed back against Victorian ideals by going out to work. They wore keys around their necks to symbolise their ownership of property. They even wore "outrageous" bloomers instead of long skirts.

Aged 24, Annie was raising a family in the poor tenements of Boston, USA. She was earning money by selling advertising space in the city's newspapers. And she was fascinated by this brave new world of bloomers and bicycles. In fact, she decided she would become the first woman to cycle around the world. There was just one problem. She had tried riding a bicycle only once before.

But she wasn't afraid. On June 7, 1894, Annie pedaled out of Boston. She carried little more than a change of clothes and a pearl-handled gun.

First stop: Chicago. It was a thousand miles away. It took Annie four months to get there. The journey was terrible. Her bike was so heavy. The roads were just rocks and sand. *The New York Times* reported she was ready to give up her trip, but that was a lie. She just swapped her bulky women's bike for a lighter man's Sterling Roadster. She turned her riding outfit into a nifty costume of leggings, sweater, cap and knickerbocker shorts. *Now* she was ready to ride, and earn lots of money.

Annie was a master saleswoman. She changed her last name from Kopchovsky to Londonderry in exchange for $100 from the Londonderry Spring Water Company. She became a human billboard, advertising everything from perfume to bicycle tires on signs and ribbons. Sailing between continents – from Europe to Africa to Asia – she sold autographs and told her travel stories to packed lecture halls. Annie's stories were about hunting Indian tigers, being locked up in Chinese prisons, and being attacked by wild pigs. Whether these stories were true or not is anyone's guess.

Bearing 40 pounds of new muscle, Annie arrived home to her husband and children on September 24, 1895.

By cycling around the globe, Annie Londonderry became a powerful symbol of changing gender roles in the United States. *The New York World* newspaper called her adventure "the Most Extraordinary Journey Ever Undertaken by a Woman."

MORE GAME-CHANGING CYCLISTS:
Dervla Murphy (b.1931, Ireland), Vedangi Kulkarni (b.1998, India)

"I am a...new woman, if that term means that I believe I can do anything that any man can do."

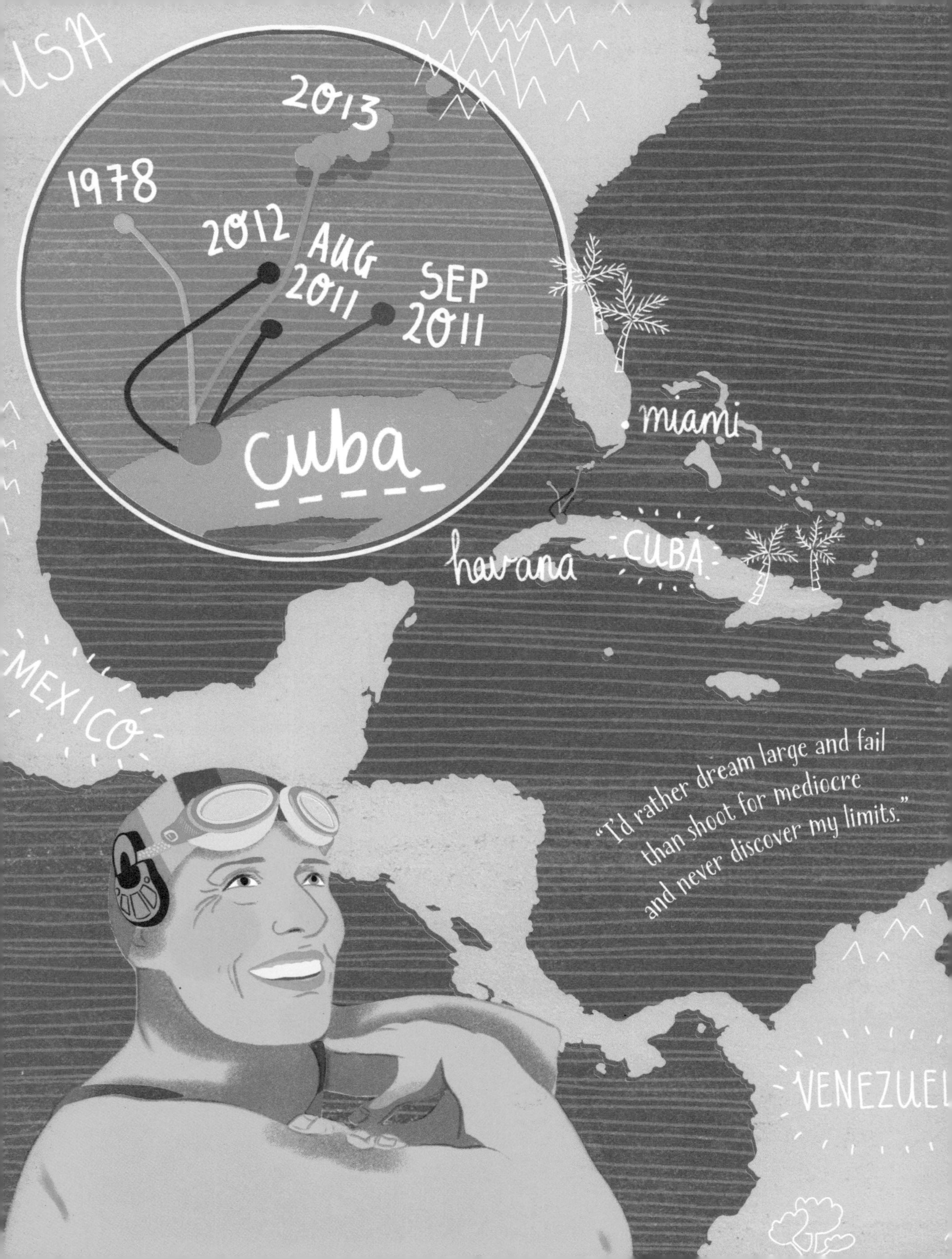

USA

2013

1978

2012 AUG
2011

SEP
2011

CUBA

miami

havana · CUBA

MEXICO

"I'd rather dream large and fail
than shoot for mediocre
and never discover my limits."

VENEZUEL

* DIANA NYAD *

The champion who swam from Cuba to Florida

1949, New York City, New York, USA

When Diana Nyad turned 60, she realized she wouldn't be around forever. While she still could, she wanted to reach for her dreams. Diana's dream had never been achieved by anyone. She wanted to be the first person to swim 111 miles without a shark cage from Havana in Cuba to Key West in Florida. That's the length of 3,574 Olympic swimming pools.

The Florida Strait is some of the most dangerous open water in the world. Since the 1950s, the world's greatest swimmers had been trying – and failing – to make the crossing. Before Diana retired from distance swimming at the age of 30, she too had tried to break the record. She failed when strong currents veered her towards Texas rather than Florida. To re-attempt the route, Diana would face sharks, storms, and the most venomous marine creature on Earth – the box jellyfish.

With her team of medics and navigators, Diana set off from Cuba in August 2011. She had no shark cage, but a kayaker with an electrical shark shield paddled by her side. When she grew hungry, the boat crew dropped food into her mouth as if she were a fish.

Twenty-nine hours into her swim, Diana had an asthma attack. The attempt was over.

Two months later, Diana made her third attempt. She was swarmed by jellyfish. The pain was so great her whole body felt like it was exploding. Forty-one hours in, she had to be pulled out of the water.

The next year, Diana made her fourth attempt. To protect herself from box jellyfish, she covered her entire face and body. Only her lips and nostrils were exposed. The jellyfish just went for her lips. After the agony faded, she picked up her stroke again. Lightning lashed the sky. Diana kept swimming. Jellyfish stung her again. She didn't stop. Her boat crew feared the kayaker by her side would be hit by the storm. Diana couldn't put someone else's life in danger. She pulled out.

On August 31, 2013, Diana started swimming towards Florida for the fifth time. This time her lips were covered by a silicone mask. This time, she had emailed her team beforehand: "We will not, under any circumstances, interrupt the swim for storms this year." Diana swam for 52 hours without sleeping. To pass the time, she thought about the four billion stars that spilled overhead in the pitch-black night. She dreamed of dancing the foxtrot on *Dancing with the Stars*. She kept swimming until 1:55 p.m., September 2, 2013.

Staggering triumphantly onto Smathers Beach, through saltwater-swollen lips, Diana said to the waiting crowd at Key West, "Never, ever give up!" She was 64 years old.

MORE RECORD-BREAKING ENDURANCE SWIMMERS:
Gertrude Ederle (first woman to swim across the English Channel, 1926),
Lynne Cox (first woman to swim between the United States and the Soviet Union, now Russia), 1987

* CHERYL STRAYED *

The writer who sparked a hiking revolution

1968, Spangler, Pennsylvania, USA

Cheryl Strayed had always dreamed of being a writer. But life was not going as planned. At 26, she was working as a waitress in Minnesota, USA. She had also thought her favorite person – her mother – would live forever. When she died of lung cancer aged 45, Cheryl was devastated.

While waiting in line at an outdoor gear store one day, Cheryl was feeling sad. Then she noticed a book cover. The photograph showed a sparkling lake surrounded by snowy mountains and blue sky. It looked close to paradise. That book was a hiker's guide to the Pacific Crest Trail. Cheryl decided to make a big change to her life. In the spring of 1995, she took a bus to Southern California. She began to hike the trail from the book.

The PCT runs for 2,650 miles between Mexico and Canada. Cutting through the mountains, desert and canyons of the American West, it's wild and spectacular. It was the challenge Cheryl was looking for.

So, Cheryl walked. When six of her toenails came off because her boots were too small, she kept walking. When her backpack felt too heavy to lift, she sighed and tried again. When the trail felt like an ascent up one long mountain, she staggered onwards. There was only one way to go. Forward. Cheryl slept in her dinky blue tent whenever she grew tired. She cooked dried rice for dinner on her stove. She thought about her past, and what she wanted for her future. As weeks turned to months, Cheryl's muscles grew. Her body became tanned and hairy. She felt strong – inside *and* out.

Three months after setting off, Cheryl reached the Bridge of the Gods between Oregon and Washington state. She had walked 1,100 miles of the Pacific Crest Trail. Walking alone had changed her perspective. Cheryl no longer felt sad or lost. She felt fierce and humble, like she was now safe in the world.

> "Fear, to a great extent, is born of a story we tell ourselves, and so I chose to tell myself a different story from the one women are told. I was strong. I was brave. I decided I was safe."

Cheryl's confidence grew so much on that trip. She decided that from then on, she would concentrate on the thing she loved most: writing. One of her books was a memoir. She named it *Wild*. It was all about her trip along the Pacific Crest Trail. *Wild* became a No. 1 *New York Times* bestseller. Then it became a hit feature film starring Reese Witherspoon. Since the release of *Wild*, more than 10 times the regular number of hikers have tried walking the full length of the Pacific Crest Trail. Cheryl has sparked a hiking revolution.

Now women everywhere know the beauty to be found in hiking and camping. They know how it feels to go beyond your comfort zone and get comfortable there. They know how to tap directly into the understanding that every single one of us is connected.

MORE LONG-DISTANCE HIKERS:
Emma "Grandma" Gatewood (1887–1973, USA), Rahawa Haile (b.1985, USA)

* KIMI WERNER *

The freediving chef who rode a shark

1980, Maui, Hawaii, USA

Kimi Werner grew up in a little cottage in tropical Maui, Hawaii. Living in the countryside, her childhood chores were a little more exciting than other children's. She collected eggs from the garden chickens. To collect the mail, she rode her pet pig down a dirt road to the letter box. And when her father caught dinner by spearfishing in the Pacific Ocean, Kimi joined him.

In her 20s, Kimi left home and began working as a chef in the city. Life was good, but she always felt like something was missing. When had life last felt fulfilling? Kimi realized it was as a child, playing in the ocean. To get back out in the water, she took up spearfishing and freediving.

The human breath is a short moment of time – about four seconds. A freediver stretches that moment into minutes. With careful training, she learns how to explore the underwater world without oxygen tanks or scuba gear. She starts each dive by slowing her breathing rate. She takes calm, deep breaths in. Out. In. Out. Her heart rate decreases. Her body relaxes. Then she plunges into the water.

When you dive deep, you feel great pressure squeezing your body. That's because water is nearly 800 times denser than air. But to Kimi, the pressure feels cosy, like a hug. Holding her breath in the water for up to five minutes, she goes spearfishing for octopus, snapper and silver wahoos. She's so good at what she does that in 2008 she won the US national spearfishing championships.

In 2013, Kimi was on a shark research expedition in Mexico. Under the water, she came face-to-face with the largest great white shark she had ever seen. It was 17 feet long, and it was coming straight towards her. Kimi let out a squeal. She began swimming in the shark's direction. All of her years in the water had taught her how to read the body language of marine creatures. The way the shark's fins were out, the way it was moving showed Kimi that this shark was good-natured. It was curious. It was just like her. Kimi reached her hand out and gently touched the shark's fin. Then the pair went for a swim!

A spearfisher and freediver, Kimi is as close to being a real-life mermaid as it gets. But in another life, she wouldn't like to come back as an ocean creature. She'd love to be an *iwa* bird. It gets to dive into the water in search of fish to eat. It also gets to soar high above in the sky!

MORE CHAMPION FREEDIVERS:

Tanya Streeter (b.1973, Cayman Islands), Sofía Gómez Uribe (b.1992, Colombia)

"Adventure means that you let your curiosity lead you into the unknown and you take the wild turns and lessons that come with it. It will rarely be easy, but you will always grow!"

* SILVANA LIMA *

The surfer who refuses to take "no" for an answer

1984, Paracuru, Brazil

Silvana Lima grew up in a shack on the beach in northern Brazil. Every day she dreamed of living in a real house, in a neighborhood where there were other children her age to play with. Still, there was one good thing about where she lived. Every week, broken surfboards washed up on the beach. Small but determined, Silvana went out and tried surfing when she was seven years old. Practising with her brothers, Silvana developed a new style. She did perfect turns on the waves. She pulled off huge jumps most men can only dream of doing.

By the time she was 22, Silvana was ranking as one of the best female surfers on the planet. But in Brazil, it wasn't easy for a woman to find a place in the water. They were told their place was on the beach, looking good. They were told it was too dangerous for women. They were told they didn't have the strength to deal with the changing nature of the ocean.

Silvana didn't believe any of that. But despite being one of the most powerful athletes around, she wasn't considered "pretty" enough to get a full sponsorship deal from a surfwear brand. Without sponsorship money, Silvana couldn't afford to compete at championships abroad. She wondered if she should make herself more attractive by dyeing her hair blonde. Maybe she could wear contact lenses to make her eyes blue. Then she would look more like the girls in the surf ads. But then no one would recognize her. It wouldn't be her. So Silvana began breeding French bulldogs. The money she made from them funded her entry into pro surf competitions.

Silvana decided to speak up. She told the BBC, "When it comes to female surfers, the brands want both models and surfers. So if you don't look like a model, you end up without a sponsor. You're excluded. You're disposable. Men don't have these problems."

> "To be inside the water, that huge expanse of water, it's a wonderful sensation."

In the end, Silvana didn't need to wear contact lenses or dye her hair to own the breaks. She just had to promote what's beautiful: passion and integrity. Today, if you spot some epic waves off the coast of New Zealand or Hawaii, look out for a 5-foot-4 woman doing huge jumps in the air. It might just be Silvana Lima. Look closely again, this time at her rash guard. Does it have a name and logo on it? One of the biggest brands in South America has put its name behind this legendary surfer.

MORE AMAZING SURFERS:
Princess Ka'iulani (1875–1899, Hawaii), Rell Sunn (1950–1998, Hawaii)

* ARUNIMA SINHA *

The amputee athlete who climbed Mount Everest

1986, Uttar Pradesh, India

Arunima Sinha climbed Mount Everest at the age of 26, but her story is a little different from the 4,000 or so others who have reached the snowy peak. Two years before her climb, thieves threw Arunima from a moving train headed to New Delhi, India. As she was scrambling off the tracks, she was hit by a train going in the opposite direction. Her left leg had to be removed at the hospital.

Injuries like this can be devastating. Arunima was on her way to a career with the police. She could not imagine giving up on all her dreams. She could not imagine being limited and defined by an injury. While recovering, she decided she would not be pitied for what had happened. "*Main* Everest *karungi*," she vowed in Hindi, "I will climb Everest."

With lots of practice, Arunima began to walk again. She even learned to rock climb with an artificial leg. Two years after her accident, she was ready to attempt the world's tallest mountain.

Imagine how high you are when you fly in a plane. That's the height Everest sits at. At nearly 30,000 feet above sea level, the air near the mountain top has very little oxygen in it. Climbers have to go very slowly and climb in short bursts. They must let their bodies adapt by taking long rests. This is called acclimatization. Arunima spent more than a month at Everest Base Camp letting her body acclimatize. Finally, at 6 p.m. on May 20, 2013, the weather cleared. It was time to go.

Because of her leg, Arunima was slower than the others in her group. Her team leader worried that she was using up her energy and oxygen levels too quickly. He told her to turn back, but she refused. She continued the crawl along narrow ridges. Step by step, Arunima dug her climber's axe into ice sheets and hoisted her way up the mountain. Near the peak she got a big burst of energy.

"When I reached the summit, I felt like screaming at the top of my voice...Here I am!"

At 10:55 a.m. on May 21, 2013, Arunima Sinha did it. She became the first female amputee to reach the top of the world. She was so happy she wanted to scream. But she still had to descend. She could feel her artificial limb coming loose from the strain. She couldn't take off her gloves and put it back in place. If she did her fingers might freeze. Instead she dragged her left foot across ice fields all the way to Base Camp.

Arunima's story of beating the odds is far from over. Dedicating her climbs to those who lose hope, she's just finished climbing the tallest mountains on all seven continents.

MORE EVEREST CLIMBERS:
Junko Tabei (first woman to reach the summit, 1975),
Pasang Lhamu Sherpa (first Nepalese woman to reach the summit, 1993)

* MIRA RAI *

The soldier running the world's most challenging trail races

1988, Jumla, Nepal

Mira Rai grew up in a remote village in the rippling green mountains of eastern Nepal. When she was 12, she had to leave school because her parents could no longer afford the fees. From then on, every day looked the same. Mira worked in the fields. She watched over the goats. There was no excitement in her life.

Aged 14, Mira ran away from home to join the Maoist guerrilla army. She liked the way they were trying to create a more equal society for men and women. At a secret jungle camp, she spent three years training in martial arts and running. When the army disbanded, Mira did not go back to her village. She moved to Nepal's capital city of Kathmandu and continued to practice running.

"I keep going, just keep going!"

In the spring of 2014, Mira was training with friends in the hills that edge the city. Mira did not know it, but an ultramarathon was taking place on the trails that day. She was in no way prepared for a 31-mile long competition. She had not even brought food or water with her. Mira competed anyway. When her pace began to slow, a bystander brought her noodles and fruit juice. Finishing in nine hours, she won the women's division.

Mira was hooked. Later that year, she ran an eight-day race through Nepal's high-desert Mustang region. She won. She ran the 50-mile Mont Blanc ultramarathon in France. Again, she won. Since then, she has raced all over the world – in Hong Kong and Italy, Scotland and New Zealand.

The ultramarathons Mira competes in are a bit like cross-country races, except they're really, *really* long and the trails are really, *really* rugged. They take place on mountain ranges, and can be more than a week long. There are aid stations where runners can drink water and slurp down energy gels, but in the very toughest competitions, trail runners have to carry their own sleeping bags, water and compass in case they get lost.

These days, Mira is a big celebrity in Nepal. Her winnings and sponsorship deals have changed her life. They have allowed her to buy a little farm and 200 chickens. Her younger siblings can now afford to go to school. Her parents no longer need to worry about where their next meal will come from.

Despite the hard work involved in training, Mira loves long-distance running. She knows she's lucky to be able to chase her goals. In her country, women don't often get to have big adventures. Mira's hope is that Nepalese women and girls get more opportunities. That's why she has launched a race series in Nepal that inspires local women to run.

MORE ENDURANCE RUNNERS:
Mirna Valerio (b.1975, USA), Aziza Raji (born *c.* 1988, Morocco)

* LAURA DEKKER *

The teenager who sailed solo around the earth

1995, Whangarei, New Zealand

Laura Dekker grew up on boats. In fact, she was born in New Zealand during her parents' own round-the-world sailing trip. Once Laura was five, it was time for her to go to school in the Netherlands.

On weekends, Laura kept sailing. After school, she practiced tying knots and hoisting sails. By the age of 14, she was sailing solo between the Netherlands and England. It was the greatest feeling. Laura thought to herself, "Why not keep going around the world?"

Laura's family supported her dream. The Dutch authorities did not. They said a 14-year-old girl was incapable of looking after herself. Laura had to defend her right to sail solo in six court cases. Journalists around the globe discussed the risks of a child sailing alone across stormy seas. Laura hated the attention. She just wanted to achieve her dream.

After a year of court battles, Laura finally won her case. So long as she did her schoolwork, she was free to sail. Laura's boat was 33 years old. It was so little that she named it *Guppy*. Her cupboards were stocked with cornflakes, powdered milk and canned beans. Her schoolwork was downloaded on her laptop. Her radar was ready to warn her of oncoming ships. The satellite phone could be used to make calls in an emergency.

On January 20, 2011, Laura set sail from the Caribbean island of St Maarten. As she crossed the world's oceans, she learned to surf and how to dive. She teased flying fish from her salt-filmed hair. She watched in amazement as pods of dolphins played in *Guppy's* wake. Sometimes, the water was so flat the stars reflected like a mirror. Other times, it was so stormy that *Guppy* and Laura were plunged deep into the churning waves. Luckily, she was always clipped to a lifeline.

> "If it doesn't challenge you, it won't change you."

Sailing around the world alone, Laura learned so much: how to sew torn sails and how to bake bread; how to shower in rainwater and keep an eye out for pirates in the Indian Ocean. Most of all, she learned about herself. Spending endless days alone, Laura realized that beauty is in life's quiet moments. It's in watching the sunset, or funny shapes in the passing clouds. It's in the passages of a book. It's in playing guitar or dancing to a song. It's in creating the life you want for yourself.

On January 21, 2012, Laura sailed into Simpson Bay on St Maarten. She had sailed the globe alone. All her friends and family were on the beach to greet her, but her journey was never about setting records. It was about the love of sailing. So she kept going – all the way to New Zealand!

MORE ROUND-THE-WORLD SAILORS:
Krystyna Chojnowska-Liskiewicz (b.1936, Poland), Ellen MacArthur (b.1976, England)

FIJI

WHANGĀREI

DARWIN

DURBAN

PORT ELIZABETH

CAPE TOWN

ST. MAARTEN

PANAMA

GALÁPAGOS ISLANDS

MARQUESAS ISLANDS

* ASHIMA SHIRAISHI *

The teenager being called the best rock climber of all time

2001, New York City, New York, USA

Rock climbing isn't as simple as going up a ladder. You can't just use the strength in your arms to go wherever you want. You must use and move every part of your body – your core, your shoulders, your fingers, legs, feet. To climb, you must *dance*. And that's exactly what Ashima Shiraishi does. She swings between crevices in the rock that can barely be seen. She does it so well she's been called the best rock climber on the planet.

Ashima was six years old when her love of climbing began. Her father, Poppo, had taken her to a playground in New York's Central Park. Ashima noticed some adults scaling the rocks nearby. She ran over to have a try. By the age of seven, Poppo was taking her to local climbing gyms. Aged eight, Ashima was setting records as the youngest person to complete climbs around the globe.

Professional athletes don't get to the top by accident. It takes time, dedication and determination. While Ashima was at high school, her days began at around 6:30 a.m. At 3 p.m. the last bell rang. Then she practiced at the climbing gym for around five hours. At 8 p.m., Ashima would go home to her family's small loft in Manhattan's garment district. She had dinner. She did her homework. At midnight, it was time for bed before starting all over again.

Ashima's life isn't all work. She loves painting, hip hop, street fashion and hanging out with her friends. She also really, really loves Japanese desserts. But she's grabbing titles for being the first to make huge climbs everywhere from Spain to Australia.

> "Climb through your problems. Failure is a huge part of success."

Her climbing career is a family affair. Poppo was a punk dancer, but now his role is to accompany Ashima on her climbing trips around the world. His job is to hold the rope that will protect his daughter if she falls. Ashima does fall, but she isn't afraid of those failures. She sits back, looks at the problem in front of her, then gets back up on the wall.

Ashima's name could soon be even bigger. At the 2020 Summer Olympics in Japan, climbing will be a sport for the first time. By then, Ashima will be 19. Is she excited? Yes. She can't wait for the chance to compete next to talented women from all over the world.

MORE REVOLUTIONARY ROCK CLIMBERS:
Barbara Zangerl (b.1988, Austria), Sasha DiGiulian (b.1992, USA)

ANADA
ARCTIC OCEAN
RUSSIA
THE NORTH POLE
Camp Barneo
Svalbard
GREENLAND
KANGERLUSSUAQ
ISORTOQ HUT
SOUTH AMERICA
Falkland Islands
RONNE ICE SHELF
ANTARCTICA
SOUTH POLE
SHACKLETON GLACIER
THE AMUNDSEN COAST
ROSS ICE SHELF

* JADE HAMEISTER *

The polar explorer who hit back at bullies from the South Pole

2001, Melbourne, Australia

Jade Hameister lives in Australia. Her birth country is famous for beaches, kangaroos and koalas. It's not so famous for snow. Yet when Jade was 12 years old, she decided to become a skier. In fact, she wanted to ski at the North Pole.

To ski in the Arctic requires lots of training, but Jade didn't have anywhere to practice her technique. Still, she could build her strength and endurance at the gym. She also went to the local beach and ran with giant tires attached to her waist. In this way, she mimicked the weight of pulling a heavy sledge across ice. By the age of 14, Jade was ready for her adventure.

> "It's so much more fun to try and be more, rather than less."

The world's far north is not a blank canvas of soft snow. At the North Pole, Jade had to navigate ice rubble. Between drifting fields of ice, there were rivers of freezing water to cross. Jade and her team had to use their sledges to build makeshift bridges over the water! Every part of Jade's body felt frozen and sore, but she never thought of giving up. She just felt lucky to be in this fragile yet stunning part of the planet.

In April 2016, after skiing 62 miles, Jade made history. She became the youngest person in history to ski to the North Pole by this route. Thirteen months later, she broke another record. In June 2017, Jade became the youngest woman to complete the 342-mile crossing over the Greenland icecap.

Jade gave a talk about her skiing adventures. On stage in Melbourne, she said that every human body is astonishing. It doesn't matter what it looks like in selfies. What matters is who we *are*. The whole audience cheered. But when the video was posted on YouTube, some male commenters wrote mean things like, "Make me a sandwich." This is a catchphrase used by internet bullies to try and make women feel small. It means, "Your achievements don't matter. Your place is at home in the kitchen."

Jade's next skiing adventure was to the South Pole. For more than a month, storms blew across the mountains of Antarctica. Jade and her team pushed on to the bottom of the world anyway. Finally, standing in her pink snowsuit under a bright sky, Jade had her photo taken. She was holding a plate with a sandwich on it. It was for her internet bullies! Jade posted the picture online. She captioned it, "I made you a sandwich (ham & cheese). Now ski 37 days and 600km to the South Pole and you can eat it."

MORE POLAR ADVENTURERS:
Ann Bancroft (b.1955, USA), Jane Francis (b.1956, England)

THE SEEKERS
Women who have journeyed in search of meaning, love, safety — the things that make a life.

1. ISABEL GODIN
2. HESTER STANHOPE
3. ALEXANDRA DAVID-NÉEL
4. ISABELLE EBERHARDT
5. ROBYN DAVIDSON
6. MANON OSSEVOORT
7. NUJEEN MUSTAFA

✳ ISABEL GODIN ✳

The noblewoman who became lost in the Amazon rainforest

1728, Riobamba, present-day Ecuador – 1792, Saint-Aman-Montrond, France

As a teenage girl from a noble Spanish family living in South America, Isabel Godin had two options in life. She could marry a man, or she could become a nun and marry God. Isabel chose to marry a French mapmaker named Jean Godin.

In 1749 Jean left what's now called Ecuador on a short trip. Because he was French, not Spanish, the authorities refused to let him return. Isabel was stuck in Spanish territory on the Pacific side of South America. Jean was stuck on the Atlantic side in French Guiana. Three thousand miles of river and rainforest kept them apart. Isabel decided that if her husband couldn't come to her, she would go to him. It took her many years to raise the funds for her trip across the continent. Eventually, she sold her home. In October 1769, she set off with guides and her brothers, to be reunited with her husband. She was 41.

Isabel and her crew traveled over the Andes. They descended into cloud forest thick with moss and orchids. Isabel was sleeping outside for the first time in her life. She was traveling among waterfalls and toucans and fruit crows. It was amazing. Then the group began canoeing along the green-brown waters of the Bobonaza River. Isabel watched turtles drift by on logs. Baby capybaras (a sort of giant guinea pig) played on the mud banks. Everything was beautiful...until it wasn't. Waking up on a sandbank one morning, Isabel couldn't see her guides. They had fled.

Isabel and her brothers were stranded. With no compass, map or food, they hacked their way through the jungle in search of help. Soon, they were lost in a gloomy world of biting flies and creeping vines. Soon, they were starving.

Women typically have a higher proportion of body fat than men. This means they often live longer in starvation situations. After four weeks in the soaking jungle, Isabel's brothers died of hunger. Now she was all alone. Isabel was so exhausted she had to drag her body across the forest floor to get anywhere. She found wild birds' eggs to eat. She licked water droplets from plants. She tried not to think of man-eating snakes or the big cats that roamed the jungle. After nine days, Isabel came across a stream. That stream turned into a river. She had found her way back!

> ## "I found myself in that difficult and sorrowful situation."

By the riverbanks, Isabel was discovered by a group of Canelos-Quichua people. They nursed her back to health, then – for five months – Isabel continued along the Amazon. On reaching French Guiana, she was reunited with Jean. It had been 21 years since they had last seen each other. Isabel and Jean stayed together for the rest of their lives, though they never did go back to Ecuador.

MORE RAINFOREST ADVENTURERS:
Kris Tompkins (b.1950, USA), Kira Salak (b.1971, USA)

* HESTER STANHOPE *

The gentlewoman who became Queen of the Desert

1776, Sevenoaks, England – 1839, D'joun, Lebanon

When Hester Stanhope was a girl, she told her uncle William Pitt the Younger that she wouldn't marry until she found someone as clever as she was. William said he knew lots of clever people. After all, he was the British Prime Minister. But if Hester was looking to find someone as intelligent as her, she would always be single.

Hester never did marry. After William died in 1806, she left England in search of new horizons. The Napoleonic Wars were raging across Europe, so she could not go to fashionable Paris or Rome. Instead she traveled to Gibraltar and Athens, Constantinople (now Istanbul, the capital of Turkey) and on to the Middle East.

> "I like traveling of all things. It is a constant change of ideas."

While sailing to Cairo, a storm shipwrecked Hester on the Mediterranean island of Rhodes. With all her belongings gone, she borrowed clothing, but she didn't want to wear the veil Ottoman women wore. She put on a man's robe and turban instead. When Hester finally arrived in Egypt, she made her outfit even jazzier with a jewelled dagger, pistols and a sword.

From there, Hester traveled to Syria. She wanted to visit the seat of an ancient royal: Queen Zenobia. A descendant of Queen Cleopatra, Zenobia was born in 3 CE and had her own mighty empire, the Palmyrene, which conquered Egypt. The ruins of Zenobia's city, Palmyra, sat deep in the Syrian Desert. Many curious travelers had been robbed and left to die in the sand on the journey there. If Hester reached the ancient city, she'd be the first European woman to make it. Riding towards the city on horseback, Hester was protected by 70 paid guards who carried long lances plumed with ostrich feathers. On reaching Palmyra, locals crowned her "Queen of the Desert." She wasn't just respected. She was worshipped.

While traveling, Hester came across a medieval document. It said that three million gold coins were buried at the ancient city of Ashkelon in Palestine. Who wouldn't love to find hidden treasure? She led a full team on an archeological dig. Her team found no gold, but they did uncover a seven-foot-tall marble statue of a Roman warrior.

In the 1820s, Hester moved into an old monastery at the foot of Mount Lebanon. She vowed never to return to England and its "boot-whipping, silly visiting people – not even for £100,000 a year." She never did go home. When Lebanon collapsed into civil war in the 1820s, hundreds of families came to "Queen Hester" for food and shelter. In the end, she took in more than a thousand refugees.

MORE GUTSY HEIRESSES:
Aimée Crocker (1864–1941, USA), Louise Boyd (1887–1972, USA)

* ALEXANDRA DAVID-NÉEL *

The Buddhist opera singer who entered the forbidden city of Lhasa

1868, Paris, France — 1969, Digne-les-Bains, France

When Alexandra David-Néel met the Dalai Lama in 1912, the Buddhist spiritual leader gave her one piece of advice: "Learn Tibetan." His words allowed her to go on her greatest adventure – to the forbidden city of Lhasa.

Alexandra was a born explorer. As a child growing up in Paris, her worried nannies often discovered her hiding behind the bushes in the park. As a teenager, she was already cycling alone through France and Spain. As soon as she finished school, she sailed to London to study Eastern religions. This was a fashionable interest during colonial times. For Alexandra, though, this was no hobby. She converted to Buddhism when she was 21. Alexandra studied singing in Brussels and became première cantatrice ("first singer") with the Hanoi Opera Company in what's now Vietnam. She traveled all across Asia and North Africa. All that glamor was fun for a while, but it was not for her. She moved to the tiny mountain kingdom of Sikkim. She spent the next few years meditating in a Himalayan cave.

In her 40s, Alexandra adopted a teenage monk called Aphur Yongden. He loved adventure just as much as she did. Once he was in his 20s, they set off across China just as the country was collapsing into civil war. They saw murders and battles. They bargained for passage with warriors. They traveled thousands of miles by yak, mule and horse.

On reaching the China–Tibet border in 1923, it was time for Alexandra and Yongden's biggest journey yet.

They would travel to the Tibetan capital of Lhasa. There was one issue. Europeans were barred from entering the country. To get around this, Yongden pretended to be a Tibetan monk on a pilgrimage. Alexandra pretended to be his elderly mother. To disguise herself, Alexandra dabbed black Chinese ink into her hair and plaited yak's fur into the ends. She rubbed cocoa and charcoal all over her face and hands. She topped the look off with big Tibetan hoops, a necklace made from 108 pieces of human skulls, and a greasy fur hat she found on the trail. Their disguise *had* to work. If they were discovered, they'd be kicked out of the country. To blend in, Alexandra and Yongden acted like poor pilgrims. They begged. They ate maggoty stews.

> "Who knows the flower best? The one who reads about it in a book, or the one who finds it wild on a mountainside?"

Hiking over the Himalayas was bliss. Alexandra loved the wild blue skies, the solitude, the eternal snows. Then, in a December storm, they got hopelessly lost in the mountains. That Christmas, dinner was boiled strips of Alexandra's leather boots.

Alexandra and Yongden slipped past the capital's army of guards in a dust storm. After four months of trekking, they had reached their destination. Alexandra was officially the first Western woman to go to Lhasa.

MORE MYSTIC VICTORIANS:
Helena Petrovna Blavatsky (1831–1891, present-day Ukraine), Annie Besant (1847–1933, England)

"A nomad I will remain for life, in love with distant and uncharted places."

ISABELLE EBERHARDT

The rebellious writer who explored the Sahara Desert

1877, Geneva, Switzerland – 1904, Aïn Séfra, Algeria

As a child growing up in Switzerland, Isabelle Eberhardt's father took complete control of her life. He dressed her in boys' clothing and cropped her hair short. He made her work long hours in the family garden. Isabelle was so unhappy. On lonely nights, she stared longingly out of her bedroom window. Looking out at the moonlit road, she dreamed of following it far from the edge of rainy Geneva. She dreamed of the deserts of North Africa.

When her parents died, Isabelle received no inheritance. Young, poor and female in an age when women had almost no power, she gave herself a new name – Si Mahmoud Essaadi. She dressed as a young Arab male and took the cheapest ferry from Marseilles to Algeria. In the capital of Algiers, Isabelle lived and dressed like the locals. This surprised the French colonialists who had settled there. They thought they were better than Arabic people. They would say to her, "We can understand your wearing men's clothes, but why wouldn't you dress up as a European man?"

Isabelle thought differently. She loved Algeria and its people. And she loved the Sahara. Most Europeans were not safe there, but local leaders respected Isabelle because she had learned Arabic. They also liked the mystical religious group she was part of. The Qadiriyya Muslims believed in important things, like helping the poor.

For Isabelle, roaming the desert was brilliant. The best bits of desert camping were the rituals: setting up long goatskin tents, watching the sunrise, waking early to hot, bitter coffee. She loved the sand and sharp sun. She loved riding horses across the desert and sleeping on a mat outside. She loved the oases – tiny paradises where plants and water could be found in the heart of the desert. She loved being so free.

The French colonial authorities began spying on Isabelle. They wondered what she was doing making friends with so many locals. They thought *she* must be a spy. When an Algerian man called Abdallah ben Mohammed tried to kill Isabelle with a sword in 1901, no one believed he was responsible. Everyone believed he had been paid by the French to do it. In court, Isabelle forgave Abdallah for his actions. She begged that his life be spared. It was, but the French expelled Isabelle from Algeria. Even though she had done nothing wrong, they said she was too "provocative" a presence to stay in the country. To get around the ban, she married her Algerian boyfriend, Slimane.

Isabelle became a local war reporter. She spoke up about the violence happening as Algerians tried to gain independence from France. She dedicated her life to social justice.

MORE DESERT ADVENTURERS:
Alexandrine Tinné (1835–1869, Netherlands), Gertrude Bell (1868–1926, England)

* ROBYN DAVIDSON *

The wanderer who crossed 1,700 miles of Australian desert to the Indian Ocean

1950, Miles, Australia

When Robyn Davidson turned 18, she left the Queensland cattle station where she grew up and hitchhiked south. She had always imagined the thrill of leaving everything behind and taking to the road. Now she was really doing it. Robyn joined the hippie movement in Sydney, but she really dreamed of traveling across the Australian Outback. She would go with the bare minimum. No two-way radios or special bush clothes. Just her, her dog, Diggity, and some camels to carry her things.

On a dusty morning in 1975, Robyn arrived in the remote Outback town of Alice Springs. She had $6 to her name and a plan to gather and train camels from the bush. She soon learned that these animals are fierce – and fiercely intelligent. She also learned that vet bills for camel injuries are fiercely expensive. Robyn was working odd jobs like window cleaning and bartending, but it wasn't enough to pay for those vet bills. She realized she could only finance her journey by writing about it. She accepted $4,000 in sponsorship from *National Geographic* magazine.

In the winter of 1977, Robyn set off across the heart of Australia. She carried giant water canteens, bedrolls, map holders, dog biscuits, a rifle, a wrap skirt, woolly socks, a jumper, some food, coffee, tea and something to sleep on. That was it. Walking 20 to 30 miles a day, Robyn endured torn feet, terrible heat and poisonous snakes. She also discovered that the desert is a living, varied place. Desert skies looked like rose quartz. Dunes were fuzzed silver by the wind.

Robyn rested at Aboriginal settlements along the way. At Pipalyatjara, she met an old man called Mr. Eddie. Though he and Robyn spoke different languages, they communicated through actions and laughter. They walked together for 200 miles.

After nine months of trekking, Robyn arrived at the Pacific Ocean. She slept under the sun and bathed her camels in waters so turquoise it was blinding. She felt waves of joy. She also felt achingly sad. She couldn't believe her time in the desert was over.

After a week, it was time to fly to New York City to meet with the *National Geographic* team. Among Manhattan's skyscrapers, Robyn struggled with her new identity. She shrugged off silly questions like, "Well honey, what's next, skateboarding across the Andes?" Robyn didn't want her trip to be all about her or what she had achieved. In her article, she turned her attention towards the Aboriginal people she had met in the desert. She explained that they were being forced from their land by racist government policies. Published in 1978, it was the magazine's best-selling issue in years.

MORE AUSTRALIAN ADVENTURERS:
Tarenorerer (c. 1800–1831), Molly Craig (c. 1917–2004)

AUSTRALIA

GUNBARREL HIGHWAY
GLENAYLE
WELL Nº 9
WELL Nº 6
DALGETY DOWNS
WINGAINNA
REDBANK GORGE
AREYONGA
START
DOCKER RIVER
MOUNT OLGA
GLEN HELEN TOURIST CAMP
TEMPE DOWNS
WOODLEIGH
CUNYU
WILUNA
CARNEGIE
PIPALYATJARA
FINISH
HAMELIN POOL
WARBURTON

"You are as powerful and strong as you allow yourself to be."

* MANON OSSEVOORT *

The adventurer who drove a tractor from Europe to the South Pole

1976, Vriezenveen, Netherlands

The Camino de Santiago is the oldest pilgrim route in Europe. It runs across Spain and ends at a craggy piece of land that juts into the Atlantic Ocean. During the Middle Ages, when people thought the Earth was flat, it was believed that if you went any farther than here you'd simply fall off the edge of the world.

In the summer of 2000, a 24-year-old Dutch woman named Manon Ossevoort hiked the Camino. Sitting alone at Cape Finisterre – "the edge of the world" – she was proud of herself for achieving her dream. As she watched the sunset over the water, she imagined even bigger, wilder dreams for herself. "What if I went to the South Pole in a tractor?" Impossible, she laughed.

> "To have dreams is beautiful but to see them realized is the most extraordinary feeling."

A few years later, Manon purchased a tractor. She told her family she was going to take it for a test drive – to the Eiffel Tower. She wanted to reject her mean inner voice that said, "How can you do the impossible? You've done nothing with your life." In 2005 she began the 23,612-mile drive from her home in the Netherlands to the South Pole. Manon's route would take her through

countries like Serbia and Bosnia that were just recovering from brutal wars. Then she would travel down the spine of Africa. She would trace a path from Egypt in the north to the Cape of Good Hope in South Africa. From there she could catch a ship to Antarctica.

Her family and friends were worried. Wasn't it dangerous to travel through war-torn countries? Places where people had so little? Surely she'd be robbed or worse! Manon promised to follow her grandmother's tip. If she ever needed help from people, she would go to the house in the village with the neatest curtains.

Manon traveled at walking speed – about 3 miles per hour. As she drove she saw great beauty. She explored Egypt's pyramids and the Nile River. She traveled in the Ethiopian highlands and Kenya's Masai Mara grasslands. She even slept by the shore of the biggest tropical lake in the world, Lake Victoria in Uganda. She found people everywhere to be good, generous and kind. She understood that if you keep an open mind – and maybe a tractor to spark interest – the world will be open with you, too.

In 2014, a team of seven joined Manon in Antarctica. They battled freezing temperatures as low as −56 °C. They crossed endless glacier fractures. Sixteen days and 1,500 miles later, Manon broke an extreme world record. She was the first person to travel from her home in the Netherlands to the South Pole by tractor.

MORE ANTARCTIC ADVENTURERS:
Liv Arnesen (b.1953, Norway), Felicity Aston (b.1977, England)

* NUJEEN MUSTAFA *

The teenager who journeyed from war-torn Syria in a wheelchair

1999, Manbij, Syria

Nujeen Mustafa was born with a condition called cerebral palsy. Confined to a wheelchair, she spent much of her life in a fifth-floor apartment in the Syrian city of Aleppo. There were no elevators, so she couldn't go down to the street unless someone carried her. There were no specialist schools to attend. Her connection to the outside world came through television. Nujeen learned English by watching American soap operas.

The Syrian Civil War broke out when Nujeen was 12. For a few years her family managed, but when the fighting increased they fled from Aleppo. They made it over the border into Turkey, but there wasn't enough money for everyone to reach safety in Germany. Her parents stayed in Turkey. Sixteen-year-old Nujeen and her older sister, Nasrine, went on to Europe alone.

At the Turkish coast, the sisters prepared to cross the Mediterranean Sea by dinghy. They tried not to think of all the people who had drowned making the journey before them. However, some passengers worried that Nujeen's metal wheelchair would puncture the boat. They said, "If it gets really rough, we'll toss the wheelchair out." Luckily, it never came to that. As the dinghy pulled up onto the Greek island of Lesvos, an aid worker called out, "Does anybody speak English?" Nujeen was the only person to shout out, "I do!" For the first time in her life,

she didn't feel like a burden. With her excellent English, she could act as an interpreter for other Syrians.

From there, the sisters were put in a crowded detention center in Slovenia. They had to cross the Macedonian border where people were being attacked with tear gas. Nujeen was constantly bumped around in her wheelchair on rough roads. She developed sores, but she didn't complain. She was excited to be going to new places, to see sunrises and mountains and castles, sunbaked fields, green mountains, and swallows that sliced the sky.

Near the end of their 3,500-mile journey, Nujeen felt sad. She had been in boats and planes and trains – all for the first time. She worried that now she was in Germany she would go back to being the girl stuck in her room. But in Cologne, Nujeen was finally able to attend school. She could do all the cool things she couldn't do in Aleppo, like play wheelchair basketball with other teenagers.

Nujeen misses her mother and father, who are still in Turkey, but she tries not to feel sad. When she was asked to define herself beyond labels like "refugee" and "disabled," she said, "Nujeen Mustafa is happy with who she is. She loves herself. She loves everyone else as well. Nujeen Mustafa loves life and the whole world."

MORE BRAVE YOUNG WOMEN:
Malala Yousafzai (b.1997, Pakistan), Greta Thunberg (b.2003, Sweden)

"I don't see why anyone would want to wallow in misery when there is such a beautiful world out there."

GLOSSARY

ACTIVISM

Trying to create change in society. If you've taken part in a protest or emailed your local MP asking them to take action on an issue you care about, you're an activist.

AMPUTATION

The removal of an arm or leg in an accident, because of illness, or through surgery. An amputee is a person who has had an amputation.

ANTHROPOLOGY

The study of people, their cultures, and how those cultures have developed. An anthropologist is an expert in or student of anthropology.

ASTRONOMY

The branch of science that studies space and the objects that exist within it – including the moon, the sun, the planets and stars. An astronomer is an expert in or student of astronomy.

BIOLOGY

The branch of science that studies living things. A biologist is an expert in or student of biology.

BOTANY

The branch of science that studies plants. A botanist is an expert in or student of botany.

BUDDHISM

One of the world's major religions, Buddhism emerged 2,500 years ago in North India. It is a little different from other religions in that there is no belief in a god. The focus is on love and compassion for all things. People who belong to this religion are called Buddhists.

CIRCUMNAVIGATION

The action of traveling all the way around something, like planet Earth. If you circumnavigate, you travel all the way around.

CIVIL RIGHTS

The basic rights every person has in a society, no matter their race, their religion or gender. Civil rights include the right to vote, to free speech, to a fair trial, and to a public education.

The American civil rights movement was a set of protests in the USA in the 1950s and '60s. The movement was a campaign for the civil rights African Americans were not being granted. Especially in the American South, African Americans were separated from white people because of their race. They were made to go to separate schools, public washrooms, and restaurants. They were made to sit on the back seats of public buses. Often, laws were designed so they could not vote.

The American civil rights movement worked. After many protests, the Civil Rights Act of 1964 came into being. It legally ended segregation in public places in the USA, and banned employment discrimination on the basis of race, color, religion, gender or nationality.

CIVIL WAR

A war which is fought between different groups of people who live in the same country.

COLONIALISM

A system where a powerful country directly controls and exploits a less powerful country to increase its own wealth and power. Supporters of colonialism are known as colonialists.

Modern colonialism began in the 1400s, and was led by Portuguese, then Spanish exploration of the American continents. Over the next few centuries, every major European country raced to control the most colonies, to create the biggest empire, to become the richest, most powerful nation. This was at great cost to the people who lived in the colonies.

CONCENTRATION CAMP

A prison that people are kept in not because they have committed any crime, but for political reasons. Concentration camps are associated with the Nazi Party. From 1933 until the end of World War II in 1945, the Nazis kept millions of Jews and other minorities in concentration camps where they were forced to work, often before being murdered.

DISCRIMINATION

The unfair treatment of groups of people, often because of their race, religion, gender or age.

ECOLOGY

The branch of science that studies the relationship between living things, like animals and plants, and the place where they live. An ecologist is an expert in or student of ecology.

EMANCIPATION

The process where people are granted the social or political rights they should always have been given.

ETHICAL

An ethical business is one that considers not just how much money it can make, but how it can benefit social and environmental causes.

FEMINISM

The belief that women and men should be granted the same respect, powers, and opportunities. A feminist is a person who believes in feminism.

FIELD BIOLOGY

The study of living things in the habitat they live in. A field biologist is an expert in or student of field biology.

FRENCH RESISTANCE

The collection of French movements that fought the Nazi occupation of France during World War II.

GENUS

A scientific label used to group together animals or plants with similar features. Modern humans and their close relatives belong to the *Homo* genus.

GEOLOGY

The branch of science that studies the history of Earth as recorded in rocks. A geologist is an expert in or student of geology.

GUERRILLA ARMY

An unofficial army that fights an official government army or rival guerrilla armies.

INDIGENOUS

The people who have been in a region from the earliest time, and before the arrival of other groups (like colonists).

MARCH ON WASHINGTON FOR JOBS AND FREEDOM

One of the major American civil rights movement protests. On Wednesday 28 August, 1963, 250,000 marched on Washington, DC, USA to demand civil rights for African Americans.

MARINE BIOLOGY

The branch of science that studies the things that live in oceans and other bodies of saltwater. A marine biologist is an expert in or student of marine biology.

METAMORPHOSIS

A process of transformation from a young form to an adult form with clear stages. For example, a butterfly grows into an adult in four phases: egg > caterpillar > chrysalis > adult.

MONSOON

A seasonal shift of wind from cold to warm regions. This shift can cause rains and heavy flooding in summer. In other seasons it can cause a long dry spell.

NAZI PARTY

The racist political party that ruled Germany from 1933–1945. Under the leadership of Adolf Hitler, the Nazi party persecuted and murdered an estimated six million Jews. This planned effort to destroy the Jewish people is called the Holocaust. The Nazi party also persecuted and murdered an estimated five million other minorities, including Indigenous Roma people and people belonging to the Jehovah's Witnesses religion. The Gestapo were the secret police of Nazi Germany and German-occupied Europe.

NEGOTIATION

The act of entering into discussions in order to reach an agreement. A person who negotiates is called a negotiator.

NEUROLOGY

The branch of science that studies the brain and nerves, especially the diseases that affect them. A neurologist is an expert in or student of neurology.

NOBEL PRIZE

Any of six international prizes awarded each year to people for their outstanding work in physics, chemistry, medicine, literature, economics or the promotion of peace.

NOMADIC

The act of traveling from place to place, with no fixed home. A nomad is a person who is nomadic.

PALEONTOLOGY

The branch of science that studies fossils and the evolution of life on Earth. A palaeontologist is an expert in or student of paleontology.

PILGRIMAGE

The actions of going to a sacred place for religious reasons, usually traveling a long distance to get there. A pilgrim is someone who goes on a pilgrimage.

PREJUDICE

An unfair opinion or feeling formed without knowing or considering all or any of the facts.

QUARANTINE

A period of isolation where people or animals with an infectious disease are kept apart from those who don't have the disease, until risk of the disease spreading is over.

REFUGEE

A person who has been forced to leave their country, especially because of war.

SAVANNAH

Tropical grasslands found in hot countries, often near deserts.

SEGREGATION

The action of setting someone or something apart from others.

STEPPE

Dry grasslands found in cool countries, far from the ocean, near mountains.

SUFFRAGETTE

A woman who wants the right to vote, and takes action to get that right. Suffragettes won the right for some women to get the vote in the United States in 1920 and in Canada in 1921.

Indigenous people referenced in this book include the following

Aboriginal
The Indigenous people of Australia.

Canelos-Quichua
An Indigenous people of Ecuador.

Inuit
The Indigenous people of the North American Arctic.

Iñupiat
The group of Inuit people living in the northwestern state of Alaska, USA.

Lacandón
The group of Maya people living in the Lacandón rainforest in the state of Chiapas, Mexico.

Māori
The Indigenous people of New Zealand.

Maya
The Indigenous people of southeast Mexico, Guatemala, Belize and parts of El Salvador and Honduras.

Nandi
The group of Indigenous Kalenjin people living in the Highland areas of the Rift Valley, Kenya.

Ngāpuhi
The largest tribe of Māori people, their traditional lands are in the northern part of North Island, New Zealand.

Twa
One of many Indigenous Pygmy groups that live in equatorial Africa.

A bit about geography, and how things change

Not all of the places mentioned in this book have the same name now as they did back then. Sometimes countries had one name, and then were invaded or colonized by other countries and named something else. Sometimes countries became part of other countries and stopped existing – and sometimes countries got split up to make two or more new ones! Sometimes this happened because of war, and sometimes because people spent many years talking to each other, and came to an agreement.

The maps in this book show the countries of the world as they exist right now, but when some of these women were alive they would have looked very different. When Isobel Gunn was alive there was no such country as Canada. When Sacagawea was born there were only 8 US states. Isabel Godin trekked through a South America that was mostly split in two, half ruled by Spain and half ruled by Portugal. Now South America is divided into 12 independent countries! The only part that is the same is French Guiana, which is still part of France. Even within your parents' lifetimes, new countries have been declared in Europe, Africa, Asia and all over the world.

Most of the countries and other locations mentioned in this book are called by their present-day names to make it less confusing, but if you look them up in the history books you might find that they were something very different. Our world changes all the time. It's just one of the things that makes it so amazing.

* ACKNOWLEDGMENTS *

Thank you to my agent, Jackie Kaiser. You're all the good things – generous and wise and kind. Deepest thank you, also, to Liz Culotti, Pia Singhal and everyone at Westwood Creative Artists.

Thank you to Gail Winskill, Erin Alladin and the team at Pajama Press in Toronto. Thank you, also, to Rebecca Needes and the team at AA Publishing in the UK.

Amy Blackwell, if anyone made these women and their stories come to life, it's you. I can't wait to see what you illustrate next.

For writing about these women and the eras they lived in, countless biographers, interviewers and historians. Especially: Annette Kobak, Boris Friedewald, Chris Chase, Christina Lamb, Durlynn Anema, Glynis Ridley, Helen Castor, Jean-Claude Baker, Jennifer Niven, Ken Cuthbertson, Michael King, Peter Zheutlin, Robert Whitaker and Ruth Middleton.

Thank you to Dylan, my best pal. My parents, for your love of flowers and light and birds. Grandma, Ewan, Jamie, Louise and Laura. Rowan, Luca, Magnus. Max and Amy. Mary, Kaia, Sage and Leif. Martin, for bringing stories of Zen monasteries and South American jungles to a tamed part of northeast Scotland in the '90s. You likely sparked all this.

For going on tiny adventures with me, thank you Genevieve, Louise, Mhairi, Lisa, Lesley-Ann, Justine, Lizzie, Jin, Fiona, Kayla, Pippa. Also Gavelojo.

I couldn't have written this book without the support of those who offered ideas and last-minute translations. Special thanks to June Ross, Conor O'Rourke, Kate Alvarez and Hala Sannoufi. Big thanks, also, to the @womenadventurers community. You all shaped this book.

Most of all, thank you to the next generation of girls. If anyone's showing what it looks like to be fierce and hopeful, it's you.

AILSA ROSS is an author, editor, and fact checker. Born in Scotland, she studied law with a focus on women's and human rights. Her work on the topic of inspirational women began on social media before expanding into the world of books. She lives in Alberta's Jasper National Park with her family.

AMY BLACKWELL is a freelance artist based in Nottingham, England. She works in several media including painting, printmaking, and clothing design. Her art has appeared in a variety of physical and digital settings, from magazines to Instagram. Her voracious passion for her craft is often fuelled by her fondness for pancakes.